TO MARTIN, MY ~~SPIRITUAL~~
BROTHER WHO HAS PROVIDED
ME WITH INSIGHT, WISDOM +
20+ YEARS OF LAUGHS.

T. J. would approve of what
we're doing with the Reunited
PARCELS OF AMERICA.

Your brother
Alexander.

The Jefferson Bible

THE
JEFFERSON
BIBLE

THE LIFE AND MORALS
OF JESUS OF NAZARETH

THOMAS JEFFERSON

With an Introduction by F. Forrester Church
and an Afterword by Jaroslav Pelikan

BEACON PRESS · BOSTON

Beacon Press
25 Beacon Street
Boston, Massachusetts 02108

Beacon Press books
are published under the auspices of
the Unitarian Universalist Association of
Congregations.

98   97   96   95   14   13   12   11   10

LIBRARY OF CONGRESS CATALOGING-IN-PUBLICATION
DATA
Jefferson, Thomas, 1743–1826.
The Jefferson Bible / The life and morals of Jesus of
Nazareth;
with an introduction by F. Forrester Church and an
afterword by Jaroslav Pelikan.
p.   cm.
English, French, Greek, and Latin.
Originally published: Washington, D.C. : U.S. G.P.O.,
1904.
Includes index.
ISBN 0-8070-7702-x (cloth)
ISBN 0-8070-7701-1 (paper)
1. Jesus Christ—Rationalistic interpretations.
2. Bible. N.T. Gospels—Criticism, interpretation,
etc.   3. Jesus Christ— Biography—Sources, Biblical.
4. Jesus Christ—Teachings.   5. Jesus Christ—History
of doctrines—18th century.   6. Jesus Christ—History of doctrines—19th century. 7. Bible. N.T. Gospels—Criticism, interpretation, etc.—18th century.   8. Bible. N.T. Gospels—Criticism,
interpretation, etc.— History —19th century.
I. Bible. N.T. Gospels.   II. Title.
BT304.95.J44   1989
226'.1—dc 19   88-34447

Contents

Following page 32 of "The Gospel according to Thomas Jefferson" appear facsimiles of three pages from Jefferson's own compilation: (1) the title page; (2) page 60, showing Jefferson's arrangement of the parallel passages in Greek, Latin, French, and English; (3) the first page of Jefferson's Table of the Texts.

Preface

In 1956, my father, Frank Church, won election to the United States Senate. As had been the custom since 1904, on the day of his swearing in he was presented with copy of Thomas Jefferson's Bible, *The Life and Morals of Jesus of Nazareth*. Two years later he gave the book to me.

On first reading, even to the eyes of a ten-year-old boy, Jefferson's Bible struck with the force of unexpected revelation. For instance, there was no mention of virgin birth or resurrection. From my occasional bouts with Sunday school, I knew how the Jesus story was supposed to begin (with angelic visitations and an immaculate conception), and end (the empty tomb and ascension to heaven). Being skeptical by nature and upbringing, such miracles figured prominently in my resistance to this great story's saving power. Jefferson's *Life and Morals of Jesus of Nazareth* began to change all that. A redaction of the four Gospels (Jefferson cut out and pasted together only those passages that made sense to him), his Bible unlocked the Scriptures for me, opening up a whole new world, one I have been exploring with deepening wonder ever since.

When my father gave me Thomas Jefferson's Bible, he quoted a famous passage from one of Jefferson's letters; "It is in our lives and not our words that our religion must be read." This led to our first serious discussion of religion; it also marked the first time religion made any sense to me. Later, when I sat down and actually read *The Life and Morals of Jesus of Nazareth*, I encountered a savior who was born in the usual way and died in the usual way. By Jefferson's reading, it was Jesus' unusual life on earth—made unusual by the simple eloquence of his teachings—that truly mattered. Though I have developed a deeper appreciation for the Gospels in their received form than Jefferson had, this put a bold new spin on the question of redemption, one that has stayed with me. I define religion as our human response to the dual reality of being alive and having to die. Resurrection or no resurrection, Jesus triumphed over death: he lived in such a way that his life proved worth dying for.

With the gift of Jefferson's Bible, a door opened for me that ultimately led to a vocation in religion. At Harvard Divinity School I wrote my master's thesis on Thomas Jefferson's Bible, under the supervision of George Huntston Wil-

liams, a Unitarian minister and church historian. In 1978 I completed a doctorate in religion
at Harvard University, and was called to the
ministry of All Souls Unitarian Church in New
York City, where I have served ever since. Some
thirty years ago, when I opened *The Life and
Morals of Jesus of Nazareth*, I had no idea that
Jefferson espoused a Unitarian theology, or
that he once claimed that "there is not a young
man now living in the U.S. who will not die an
Unitarian." But in retrospect I can see that the
seed of a faith that has been growing ever since
was then planted in the mind of a ten-year-old
boy.

You can imagine, therefore, what pleasure I
take in introducing Jefferson's Bible to you.
With the exceptions of an expensive scholarly
edition and a gift-shop pocket version sold at
Monticello, *The Life and Morals of Jesus of Nazareth* has been out of print, and therefore un-
available, for years. I am so very grateful to
Wendy Strothman, director of Beacon Press, for
welcoming my suggestion that Beacon repub-
lish a new edition of Jefferson's Bible, and delighted that she asked Professor Jaroslav Pelikan
of Yale University to join with me in introducing it. Ten years ago Dr. Pelikan wrote an essay
for my first publishing venture, *Continuities and
Discontinuities in Church History: Essays in Honor*

PREFACE

of George Huntston Williams on His Sixty-fifth Birthday, which I co-edited with Timothy George (Leiden: Brill, 1978). The opportunity to work with Dr. Pelikan again on a text that I first devoted careful attention to as Dr. Williams's student, represents one of those little continuities that invest my life with meaning and joy.

F. FORRESTER CHURCH

THE GOSPEL ACCORDING TO
Thomas Jefferson

F. FORRESTER CHURCH

On 17 July 1771, his neighbor Robert Skipwith asked Thomas Jefferson to propose a list of books suitable for a library befitting the dignity of a Virginia gentleman. Skipwith was prepared to invest some twenty-five or thirty pounds; he wished to have his volumes finely bound and gold-embossed. Jefferson promptly drew up a catalog of books, plainly bound, costing no less than one hundred and seven pounds, and then suggested, not unkindly, that Skipwith instead abandon the scheme, and come to his home, "the new Rowanty, from which you may reach your hand to a library formed on a more extensive plan."

When Jefferson offered the same opportunity to Congress in proposing to sell his library to replace that which had been destroyed by fire by the British during the War of 1812, Congressman Cyrus King of Massachusetts was offended. From the floor of the House he exclaimed: "It might be inferred, from the character of the man who collected it, and France, where the collection was made, that the library contained irreligious and immoral books, works of the French philosophers, who caused and influenced the volcano of the French Revolution. The bill would put $23,999 into Jefferson's pocket for about 6,000 books, good, bad, and indifferent, old, new, and worthless, in languages which many cannot read and most ought not."

More telling than King's invective was Jefferson's scheme of classification as formulated in the catalog that he submitted to Congress. Building upon the framework that Francis Bacon in 1605 had constructed in his essay, "The Advancement of Learning," Jefferson classified his books with reference to the processes of mind employed on them: (1) *Memory*, which is applied to factual data, such as "History"; (2) *Reason* (according to Bacon, *Understanding*), which is applied to theoretical investigations, such as "Philosophy"; and (3) *Imagination*, which is applied to innocent pleasures, such as the "Fine Arts." But having appropriated Bacon's three principal divisions of learning, Jefferson further adapted them to conform with modern canons of epistemology. Under "Philosophy," of the two primary subdivisions— "From Reason" and "Revealed"—only the former remains, no longer identified as such, but assumed to be guiding the "Moral" and "Mathematical" pursuits into which it has been divided. As additional evidence for the changes Jefferson worked upon Bacon's categories, "Mathematical" had previously been a third-tier subsection of "Metaphysics/Speculative"; "Natural Religion," which had stood in its place (having first been transformed by Jefferson into "Law of Nature and Nations"), now served to fill the lacuna left by "Mathematics" on the lowest rank.

One could go on, but for our purposes it need only be pointed out that Jefferson subtended "Religion" to "Jurisprudence," a category of "Philosophy/Moral," where its awkwardness suggests that he had been reluctant to ascribe to it an autonomous, if more appropriate, status. In addition, Jefferson demoted "Ecclesiastical History" from a partner to a function of "Civil History," while eliminating its more speculative subdivisions, such as "History of Providence."

To substantiate any conclusions one might draw from such schemes of subordination, we need only look to Jefferson's breakdown of authors and titles under the various headings. Since his library catalog reflects the same fundamental principles of classification illustrated

by the list of books he had proposed to Skipwith, by turning to this we may gain a clearer
notion of Jefferson's criteria. To Skipwith, under
"Religion" and shouldering Sterne's sermons,
Jefferson commended Xenophon on Socrates,
Epictetus, Antoninus, Seneca, Cicero, and, of
the moderns, Lord Kames's *Natural Religion*, Bolingbroke, and Hume. Classified under ancient
history, together with Bayle's *Dictionary* and
Plutarch's *Lives*, are Caesar, Livy, Sallust, Joseph-
us, Tacitus, *and* the Bible.

JEFFERSON'S "SYLLABUS"

As a young man, Jefferson had been much
taken by the philosophical writings of Henry
St. John, Viscount Bolingbroke. Though a Tory
in politics, Bolingbroke's religious skepticism
proved sufficiently engaging to prompt Jefferson to record passages from Bolingbroke's writings into his "Literary Bible," a commonplace
book composed during the 1760s and early
1770s. Not only do the quotations from Bolingbroke constitute by far the most extensive
entry (some sixty handwritten pages), but they
are also the only ones to treat Christianity explicitly. As an indication of Jefferson's own early
thinking on the subject of religion, one passage
of Bolingbroke's that he chose to reproduce in
his commonplace book is particularly telling.

It is not true that Christ revealed an entire body of ethics, proved to be the law of nature from principles of reason, and reaching all the duties of life.... Were all the precepts of this kind, that are scattered about in the whole new testament, collected, like the short sentences of ancient sages in the memorials we have of them, and put together in the very words of the sacred writers, they would compose a very short as well as unconnected system of ethics. A system thus collected of the writings of ancient heathen moralists, of Tully, of Seneca, of Epictetus, and others, would be more full, more entire, more coherent, and more clearly deduced from unquestionable principles of knowledge.

If Jefferson had been convinced of this in his youth, by 1803 he had begun to adjust his opinions. Although admitting that the teachings of Jesus were incomplete and had suffered badly at the hands of those who had edited them, Jefferson was now prepared to claim that the fragments remaining showed a master workman, whose "system of morality was the most benevolent and sublime ... ever taught, and consequently more perfect than those of any of the ancient philosophers." We must look to the years between for evidence that may help explain Jefferson's change of heart.

In the evenings of 1798–99, when he was John Adams's vice president, Jefferson engaged Dr. Benjamin Rush in a series of "delightful conversations ... which served as an anodyne to the afflictions of the crisis through which our country was then laboring." The Christian religion was sometimes their topic, and in the course of one discussion Jefferson promised Rush, a doctor from Philadelphia, well-respected scientist, and outspoken Universalist, that one day he would write down his view of it. In September of 1800, Jefferson wrote Rush to assure him that he had not forgotten his promise. "On the contrary," he explained, "it is because I have reflected on it, that I find much more time necessary for it than I can at present dispose of." For the moment he could only say, "I have a view of the subject which ought to displease neither the rational Christian nor Deist, and would reconcile many to a character they have too hastily rejected. I do not know that it would reconcile the *genus irritabile vatum* who are all in arms against me. Their hostility is on too interesting ground to be softened."

Jefferson was then standing as a candidate for the presidency. It was natural that his thoughts, in turning to religion, would fix on certain sectaries, the more vocal of whom were reviling him as an infidel too impious to be president. "The returning good sense of our country threatens abortion to their hopes," Jefferson wrote to Rush. "They believe that any portion of power confided to me, will be exerted in opposition to their schemes. And they believe rightly; for I have sworn upon the altar of God, eternal hostility against every form of tyranny over the mind of man."

The following spring, a triumphant Jefferson ascribed to his victory legendary proportions. "It was the Lilliputians upon Gulliver," he wrote. "Our countrymen have recovered from the alarm into which art and industry had thrown them; science and honesty are replaced on their high ground; and you, my dear Sir, as their great apostle, are on its pinnacle." This "great apostle" was Dr. Joseph Priestley, prominent scientist and Unitarian theologian.

Men like Benjamin Rush and Joseph Priestley helped to reestablish Christianity as a viable option for "reasonable" and "enlightened" republicans such as Thomas Jefferson. Historian J. B. Bury, in developing his special theme (the idea of progress), cited Priestley's doctrine of historical progress as a "solvent of theological beliefs" heralding the French philosopher Auguste Comte's Religion of Humanity. Rush, whose principal contribution to American thought was made in chemistry and medicine, also proved an ardent champion of theological openness. Urging his fellow Universalists to eschew sectarian association and include persons of every Christian society into their fellowship, he sought the establishment of an ecumenical body that would serve the interests of many in a shared and single cause. Like Priestley, Rush too believed that "all truths are related, or rather there is but one truth." As he wrote to the Reverend Jeremy Belknap in 1791, "Republicanism is a part of the truth of Christianity. It derives power from its true source. It teaches us to view our rulers in their true light. It abolishes the false glare which surrounds kingly government, and tends to promote the true happiness of all its members as well as of the whole world, for peace with everybody is the true interest of all republics." If Rush, a political ally and trusted friend, prompted Jefferson to consider incorporating a constructive Christian philosophy into his thought, Priestley suggested the means by which he might do it. By consulting the annals of history, Priestley had determined that much of Christian doctrine was either defiant of or superfluous to the Christian message. The Gospel was therefore not only obscured, but also distanced from the lives of many persons who had neither the time nor the means to investigate it properly.

Four years passed before Jefferson found the time to fulfill his promise to Rush. "The more

TO THOMAS JEFFERSON

I considered it, the more it expanded beyond the measure of either my time or information," Jefferson explained. But one day, as he was about to return to Washington from an early spring visit to Monticello, inspiration knocked. In the mail, Jefferson received from Joseph Priestley his short treatise, *Socrates and Jesus Compared.* Otherwise unoccupied for the return trip, he had occasion to peruse it. Finding the contents supportive of his own tentative conclusions, he wrote Priestley an enthusiastic reply. Alluding in the course of this letter to his promise to Rush, Jefferson sketched the form that the fulfillment of that promise might take:

I should proceed to a view of the life, character, and doctrines of Jesus, who sensible of the incorrectness of his forbears' ideas of the Deity, and of morality, endeavored to bring them to the principles of a pure deism, and juster notions of the attributes of God, to reform their moral doctrines to the standard of reason, justice, and philanthropy, and to inculcate the belief of a future state. This view would purposely omit the question of his divinity, and even his inspiration. To do him justice, it would be necessary to remark the disadvantages his doctrines had to encounter, not having been committed to writing by himself, but by the most unlettered of men, by memory, long after they had heard them from him, when much was forgotten, much misunderstood, and presented in every paradoxical shape. Yet such are the

9

fragments remaining as to show a master workman, and that his system of morality was the most benevolent and sublime probably that has been ever taught, and consequently more perfect than those of any of the ancient philosophers. His character and doctrines have received still greater injury from those who pretend to be his special disciples, and who have disfigured and sophisticated his actions and precepts, from views of personal interest, so as to induce the unthinking part of mankind to throw off the whole system in disgust, and to pass sentence as an imposter on the most innocent, the most benevolent, and the most eloquent and sublime character that ever has been exhibited to man.

Jefferson drew up his *Syllabus of an estimate of the merit of the Doctrines of Jesus, compared with those of others* sometime during the two weeks following his letter to Priestley. An enlargement upon the outline there suggested, he sent it to Benjamin Rush in fulfillment of their long-standing agreement. Four years had passed, during which, Jefferson claimed, "At the short intervals ... when I could justifiably abstract my mind from public affairs, the subject has been under my contemplation." As he had before to Priestley, Jefferson explained how, in time, his conception of the task had outdistanced his ability to accomplish it. In lieu of something more substantial, he sent his *Syllabus* to Rush, "as the only discharge of my promise I can probably ever execute."

Divided into three sections, "Philosophers," "Jews," and "Jesus," Jefferson articulated his thesis more explicitly than he had in the letter to Priestley. Of Jesus, he wrote:

1. Like Socrates & Epictetus, he wrote nothing himself.

2. But he had not, like them, a Xenophon or an Arrian to write for him. On the contrary, all the learned of his country, entrenched in its power and riches, were opposed to him, lest his labors should undermine their advantages; and the committing to writing his life and doctrines fell on the most unlettered and ignorant men; who wrote, too, from memory, and not till long after the transactions had passed.

3. According to the ordinary fate of those who attempt to enlighten and reform mankind, he fell an early victim to the jealousy and combination of the altar and the throne, at about 33 years of age, his reason having not yet attained the maximum of its energy, nor the course of his preaching, which was but of 3 years at most, presented occasions for developing a complete set of morals.

4. Hence the doctrines which he really delivered were defective as a whole, and fragments only of what he did deliver have come to us mutilated, misstated, and often unintelligible.

11

5. They have been still more disfigured by the corruptions of schismatising followers, who have found an interest in sophisticating and perverting the simple doctrines he taught by engrafting on them the mysticisms of a Grecian sophist, frittering them into subtleties, and obscuring them with jargon, until they have caused good men to reject the whole in disgust and to view Jesus himself as an imposter. Notwithstanding these disadvantages, a system of morals is presented to us, which, if filled up in the true style and spirit of the rich fragments he left us, would be the most perfect and sublime that has ever been taught by man.

In his cover letter to Rush, Jefferson described his *Syllabus* as "the result of a life of inquiry and reflection, and very different from the anti-Christian system imputed to me by those who know nothing of my opinions. To the corruptions of Christianity, I am indeed opposed; but not to the genuine precepts of Jesus himself."

Having fulfilled his promise to Rush, Jefferson turned again to Priestley. Convinced that Priestley would act upon any suggestion he might make, Jefferson commended his proposed study of Jesus' doctrines—as outlined in his *Syllabus*—to Priestley's care. That December, when Priestley agreed to investigate the matter further, Jefferson was delighted. "I have prevailed upon Priestley to undertake the work," Jefferson wrote to his daughter, Mary. "He says he can accomplish it in the course of a year." The only stumbling block was Priestley's health. "In truth his health is so much impaired," Jefferson admitted, "and his body become so feeble, that there is reason to fear he will not live out even the short term he has asked for it." A month later, in renewing his support and appreciation, Jefferson wrote to Priestley, "I rejoice that you have undertaken the task of comparing the moral doctrines of Jesus with those of the ancient Philosophers. You are so much in possession of the whole subject, that you will do it easier and better than any other person living." The letter was probably not seen by Priestley, who died within a week of its posting.

In this final letter to Priestley, Jefferson included one further bit of advice concerning Jesus, which he expected Priestley to accept without question. "I think you cannot avoid giving, as preliminary to the comparison, a digest of his moral doctrines, extracted in his own words from the Evangelists, and leaving out everything relative to his personal history and character. It would be short and precious. With a view to do this for my own satisfaction, I had sent to Philadelphia to get two testaments Greek of the same edition, and two English, with a design to cut out the morsels of morality, and paste them on the leaves of a book, in the manner you describe as having been pursued in forming your Harmony. But I shall now get the thing done by better hands."

The first intimation of Jefferson's Bible, this passage also reflects a gap between Jefferson's perception of Priestley and Priestley himself. Though both were Unitarian in theology, Priestley was far more reverent toward the Evangelists' record of Jesus' teachings than Jefferson was. Had Priestley compiled such a digest, it likely would have included every saying of Jesus recorded by the Evangelists, with the possible exception of duplications. What Jefferson failed to recognize was that, whereas Priestley doubted the genuineness of certain phenomena suggested by Scripture, he did so by showing them to be secondary to the original accounts of the Evangelists. To Priestley, the Evangelists were inspired, accurate, and trustworthy. The culprits were not Matthew, Mark, Luke, and John, but later writers, who somehow managed to graft their own speculations onto the Scriptures. Accounts of the virgin birth, for instance, clearly cut against Priestley's sense of the historical grain, but given that the story was missing from Mark, he simply concluded that the first chapters of Matthew and Luke could accordingly be dismissed as interpolations.

In exposing the corruptions of Christianity, Priestley was defending the purity of the scriptural witness. In reviling the credulous for accepting on faith unreasonable manifestations of the Spirit in later times, he was protecting the special authority of the wonderworkers whose deeds were authoritatively attested in the Testaments, Old and New. To Jefferson, on the other hand, the Evangelists were ignorant, unlettered men. If they were guilty of considerable presumption in proposing to record Jesus' life and teachings, one would be even more presumptuous uncritically to accept their accounts. Had Priestley lived, Jefferson would surely have been disappointed by Priestley's fidelity to the Evangelists' accounts of Jesus' life and teachings. But Priestley did not live, and so Jefferson determined to accomplish on his own the task he was certain Priestley would otherwise have performed to their mutual satisfaction: he himself would try his hand at cutting up the Gospels.

Shortly before importuning Priestley, Jefferson had written to a Philadelphia bookseller for duplicate copies of both the English and the Greek New Testament. The English edition was the King James translation published by Jacob Johnson in Philadelphia in 1804; the Greek, Wingrave's printing of Leusden's Greek Testament, published in London in 1794. Whether or not Jefferson intended it, the Greek text came with a parallel Latin translation (done in "a very dubious kind of Latin," in one scholar's estimation) that proved to be the work of Benedictus Arias Montanus, the Spanish editor of the Antwerp polyglot of 1569–72. Though Jefferson had expressed an interest only in the Greek with an English translation facing, when the Bibles arrived in three versions, he appears to have determined, for the sake of symmetry, to incorporate also a French translation. A year after Priestley's death, on 31 January 1805, Jefferson ordered two copies of "le Nouveau Testament corrigé sur le Grec," identical with the Paris Ostervald edition, published in 1802 under the auspices of the British and Foreign Bible Society in London. By mid 1805 Jefferson was thus in possession of the makings of his four-column *Life and Morals of Jesus of Nazareth*. The six books sat untouched on his shelves for fifteen years.

THE PHILOSOPHY OF JESUS
OF NAZARETH

The most mysterious chapter in the story of Jefferson's Bible concerns his first actual abstraction of Jesus' words from the four Gospels. Entitled *The Philosophy of Jesus of Nazareth*, this little work is first mentioned in a letter to John Adams dated 13 October 1813.

We must reduce our volume to the simple evangelists, select, even from them, the very words only of Jesus, paring off the amphiboligisms into which they have been led, by forgetting often, or not understanding what had fallen from him, by giving their own misconceptions as his dicta, and expressing unintelligibly for others what they had not understood themselves. There will be found remaining the most sublime and benevolent code of morals which has ever been offered to man. I have performed this operation for my own use, by cutting verse by verse out of the printed book, and by arranging the matter which is evidently his, and which is as distinguishable as diamonds in a dunghill. The result is an octavo of forty-six pages, of pure and unsophisticated doctrines, such as were professed and acted on by the unlettered Apostles, the Apostolic Fathers, and the Christians of the first century.

When did Jefferson perform this operation, and what has *The Philosophy of Jesus* to do with Jefferson's designs of 1803–5? The evidence from his correspondence is sketchy. "I have made a wee little book," he wrote in 1816 to his old friend, Charles Thompson, "which I call the Philosophy of Jesus. It is a paradigma of his doctrines, made by cutting the texts out of the book, and arranging them on the pages of a blank book, in a certain order of time or subject. A more beautiful or precious morsel of ethics I have never seen." A somewhat more precise reference to Jefferson's *Philosophy* appears three years later in a letter to William Short, a Unitarian with whom Jefferson maintained a correspondence concerning religion during his final years. Describing it as an "Abstract from the Evangelists of whatever has the stamp of the eloquence and fine imagination of Jesus," Jefferson reports that he attempted the task "too hastily some 12. or 15. years ago. It was the work of 2. or 3. nights only at Washington, after getting thro' the evening task of reading the letters and papers of the day." A record of his receipts indicates that Jefferson was not exaggerating. On 4 February 1804, two New Testaments (nearly identical editions published in Dublin by George Grierson in 1791 and 1799) arrived from his bookseller; little more than a month later, on March 10, Jefferson's finished work returned from the bindery.

On the cover page, Jefferson described the

contents as "an abridgment of the New Testament for the use of the Indians, unembarrassed with matters of fact or faith beyond the level of their comprehensions." As this ascription of purpose is not to be reiterated, much less elaborated, in any subsequent mention of the *Philosophy*, one must entertain it with caution. In no way is it impossible that Jefferson should have sponsored such a project. In 1809 he greeted a secular plan for civilizing the Indians as "undoubtedly a great improvement on the ancient and totally ineffectual one of beginning with religious missionaries." Once the Indians had been taught to raise cattle, to reckon value, to keep accounts, and to read, only then, stated Jefferson, should the missionaries be brought in. "Our experience has shown that this must be the last step of the process," Jefferson wrote. In the "final quarter's" instruction, Jefferson's ideal curriculum for the education of Indians might well have included an expurgated account of Jesus' doctrines.

But the evidence suggests that, when he prepared *The Philosophy of Jesus*, Jefferson's mind was more on himself than on the Indians. When alluding to the *Philosophy* in his correspondence, never once did Jefferson describe it as a collection for the Indians. "I have performed this operation for my own use," he wrote in a letter to Adams. On another occasion, Jefferson spoke of the project as an extension of ideas contained in the *Syllabus* made "for my own satisfaction." One possibility is this: in his reference to "the Indians" Jefferson was wryly alluding to his Federalist opponents. He had done so at least once before, in his second inaugural address. There he veiled a critique of his political and religious opponents with reference to the "prejudices" of the aboriginal inhabitants of America. A more likely explanation is simply that, being extremely wary of any public discussion of his private religious feelings, Jefferson was providing himself with a cover story should his *Philosophy* ever come to public notice.

In either case, Jefferson clearly viewed the *Philosophy* as but the partial fulfillment of a promise, one to be completed in *The Life and Morals of Jesus of Nazareth*, a late and, by that time, unexpected fruit of his old age. That he had intended to expand his *Philosophy* earlier, recasting it in a format that would accommodate Greek, Latin, and French texts in parallel with the English, is clear from his ordering of two French New Testaments in January 1805. But the stimulus was gone. Remember, Jefferson made his first cut at the Gospels within a week or two of hearing of Joseph Priestley's death. A year later, without Priestley to fire it further, his passion began to fade. By mid 1805, when the final set of Testaments arrived from Philadelphia, the motivation necessary to complete the work was gone. Wanting the provocation of a correspondent, Jefferson could not sustain his interest in the project. Had it not been for John Adams, who began to prod him in a remarkable correspondence initiated a decade later, *The Life and Morals of Jesus of Nazareth* would have remained an unfulfilled dream.

THE ADAMS CORRESPONDENCE

Before his letter of September 1800 to Benjamin Rush, Jefferson's published correspondence contains only one extended reference to his religious beliefs. But in the wake of his promise to Rush, a dozen more followed in the space of three and a half years, each alluding to reflections evoked by it. It is therefore fitting that after almost ten years of silence the subject of Jefferson's religious opinions again came to the fore on the occasion of Rush's death. Saddened by the loss of a close and beloved friend, Jefferson was also concerned lest, in the sorting of Rush's papers, his *Syllabus* should arouse curiosity and be indiscreetly used. To Benjamin's son, Richard, Jefferson wrote:

21

My acquaintance with him began in 1776. It soon became intimate, and from that time a warm friendship has been maintained by a correspondence of unreserved confidence. In the course of this, each had deposited in the bosom of the other communications which were never intended to go further. In the sacred fidelity of each to the other these were known to be safe: and above all things that they would be kept from the public eye. There may have been other letters of this character written by me to him: but two alone occur to me at present, about which I have any anxiety. These were of April 21, 1803 and January 16, 1811. The first of these was on the subject of religion, a subject on which I have ever been most scrupulously reserved. I have considered it as a matter between every man and his maker in which no other, and far less the public had a right to intermeddle. To your father alone I committed some views on this subject in the first of the letters above mentioned, led to it by previous conversations, and a promise on my part to digest and communicate them in writing.

Jefferson wrote this letter on 31 May 1813. Amplifying his fears, only nine days later he discovered that one of his letters to Joseph Priestley had been published without authorization in another's memoirs. The bearer of this distressing news was none other than John Adams. On this ironic note began the notable correspondence between Jefferson and Adams on the subject of religion.

While reading *The Memoirs of Theophilus Lindsey*, a British Unitarian minister, Adams happened upon Jefferson's letter to Priestley of 1803, the one in which he described his compact with Rush and commended his proposed outline of Jesus' doctrines to Priestley's care. Assuming that Jefferson had not fulfilled his pledge to Rush, Adams wrote to him, "Your letters to Priestley have increased my grief, if that were possible, for the loss of Rush. Had he lived, I would have stimulated him to insist on your promise to him, to write him on the subject of religion. Your plan I admire." Having done what he could to cajole Jefferson into contemplating such matters anew, Adams closed by announcing, "I have more to say on this subject of religion."

Two days later Adams made good on this boast. His opening salvo to Jefferson on the subject of religion is littered with credentials: the names of divines and philosophers and their books, many "whose titles you have never seen." Superficially, it appears that an insecure Adams was seeking to impress Jefferson with the breadth of his knowledge. More likely he was simply pledging his openness, his willingness to listen, his childlike delight in variety. All is summed up in Adams's closing statement: "I think I can now say I have read away bigotry, if not enthusiasm."

In the third letter of twice as many days, Adams stated his purpose clearly: "I hope you will still perform your promise to Doctor Rush." Two weeks later he reiterated that hope, including excerpts of Priestley's letter of 19 December 1803 to Lindsey, in which Priestley discusses the project suggested to him by Jefferson. "I send you this extract for several reasons," Adams wrote. "First, because you set him upon this work. Secondly, because I wish you to endeavor to bring it to light and get it printed. Thirdly, because I wish it may stimulate you to pursue your own plan which you promised to Dr. Rush."

On 22 August, Jefferson finally responded. "Since my letter of June the 27th, I am in your debt for many; all of which I have read with infinite delight. They open a wide field for reflection, and offer subjects enough to occupy the mind and pen indefinitely." Jefferson was particularly pleased by Adams's approval of his outline to Priestley. "Your approbation of my outline to Dr. Priestley is a great gratification to me," he wrote. The case was again open.

Adams's prodding brought Jefferson's *Life and Morals of Jesus of Nazareth* one step closer to fruition.

THE LIFE AND MORALS OF
JESUS OF NAZARETH

How and when Jefferson finally created *The Life and Morals of Jesus of Nazareth* is nowhere made explicit. The *Philosophy* was first mentioned during the correspondence with Adams, and then again in the letter to Charles Thompson in January of 1816. In the spring of that same year, Francis Adrian van der Kemp, a Dutch scholar and Unitarian minister, having been shown the *Syllabus* when visiting John Adams, wrote to Jefferson inquiring after it. At some point during this same period, Jefferson seems to have recommitted himself to his original task.

"If I had time," Jefferson wrote to Charles Thompson, "I would add to my little book the Greek, Latin and French texts, in columns side by side." That was in January of 1816. By April of the same year, Jefferson had elected the coming winter as the time during which he would complete his design. "It was too hastily done," he wrote, ". . . being the work of one or two evenings only, while I lived at Washington, overwhelmed with other business, and it is my intention to go over it again at more leisure. This shall be the work of the ensuing winter."

Failing to find time for it that winter, Jefferson seems, once again, to have abandoned any hope of completing his design. Three years later, he wrote to William Short, "These are now idle projects for me. My business is to beguile the wearisomeness of declining life, as I endeavor to do, by the delights of classical reading and of mathematical truths, and by the consolations of a sound philosophy, equally indifferent to hope and fear."

Whatever drove him out of his idleness long enough, first to revise the *Philosophy*, and further, to cut out the passages and paste them in a book, is nowhere made explicit. Most scholars give 1819 as the probable time of its execution, but given Jefferson's mood of late October that year, this is less likely than a subsequent date. For a more reasonable estimate, we must turn to Jefferson's additional correspondence with Short.

One hypothetical reconstruction of the chronology is as follows. As was the case before with Priestley, Adams, and Van der Kemp, upon learning of Jefferson's *Syllabus*, his friend William Short requested a copy in March 1820. Responding to this request, Jefferson had occasion to review the *Syllabus*, and consequently to assess its inadequacy as a guide for his present thoughts. He then determined to revise the *Philosophy*, partly to clarify in his own mind which of the sayings extracted before from the Gospels would survive a more deliberate scrutiny. He was well advanced in this process by the thirteenth of April, when he forwarded the *Syllabus* to Short. In the body of the covering letter, for the first time in sixteen years he spoke of restoring the Scriptures to their original purity, without expressing dissatisfaction with his first attempt (or even mentioning it), as had heretofore been his custom in correspondence whenever the subject arose. In addition, Jefferson now distanced himself from the opinions of Jesus as outlined in the *Syllabus*, indicating a new flurry of activity and reflection. In his covering letter, he wrote to Van der Kemp:

While this syllabus is meant to place the character of Jesus in its true and high light, as no imposter Himself, but a great Reformer of the Hebrew code of religion, it is not to be understood that I am with Him in all His doctrines. I am a Materialist; He takes the side of Spiritualism. He preaches the efficacy of repentance towards forgiveness of sin; I require a counterpoise of good works to redeem it, etc., etc. It is the innocence of His character, the purity and sublimity

of His moral precepts, the eloquence of His inculca-
tions, the beauty of the apologues in which He con-
veys them, that I so much admire; sometimes, indeed,
needing indulgence to eastern hyperbolism. My eu-
logies, too, may be founded on a postulate which all
may not be ready to grant. Among the sayings and
discourses imputed to Him by His biographers, I find
many passages of fine imagination, correct morality,
and of the most lovely benevolence; and others,
again, of so much ignorance, so much absurdity, so
much untruth, charlatanism and imposture, as to
pronounce it impossible that such contradictions
should have proceeded from the same Being. I separate, therefore, the gold from the dross; restore to
Him the former, and leave the latter to the stupidity
of some, and roguery of others of His disciples.

Jefferson's opinions on Jesus and the Evangelists are sharper than ever before. Judging
from the rhetoric of his letters, he is increasingly impatient with Jesus' biographers, yet his
selections in this second compilation are more
encompassing of biographical details in Jesus'
life. These two developments—Jefferson's
growing distrust of the Evangelists' account and
his growing interest in Jesus' life as well as his
teachings—began with the Adams correspondence of 1813–14. This led to his decision to
revise the *Philosophy* in 1816, and culminated,
most likely, during the spring of 1820 with the
composition of the *Life*. This last conjecture is

based upon the second and third of Jefferson's letters to Short. As can be seen from the passage just cited, we meet a significant change of tense in those sentences that describe the process of extraction: "I find, . . . separate, . . . restore, . . . leave." One senses here either present or recent involvement in the task.

In a third letter to Short, mailed on 4 August, there is even stronger evidence that the work has finally been done and is fresh in mind.

We find in the writings of [Jesus'] biographers matter of two distinct descriptions. First, a groundwork of vulgar ignorance, of things impossible, of superstitions, fanaticisms and fabrications. Intermixed with these, again, are sublime ideas of the Supreme Being, aphorisms, and precepts of the purist morality and benevolence, sanctioned by a life of humility, innocence, and simplicity of manners, neglect of riches, absence of worldly ambition and honors, with an eloquence and persuasiveness which have not been surpassed. These could not be the intentions of the groveling authors who related them. They are far beyond the powers of their feeble minds. They show there was a character, a subject of their history, whose splendid conceptions were above suspicion as being interpolations from their hands. Can we be at a loss in separating such materials and ascribing each to its original author? The difference is obvious to the eye and to the understanding, and we may read as we run to each his part; and I will venture to affirm

that he who, as I have done, will undertake to win-
now this grain from the chaff, will find it not to require a moment's consideration. The parts fall asunder of themselves, as would those of an image of
metal and clay.

Here Jefferson can look back upon a work
accomplished, not one hastily completed some
sixteen years before, with which he was no
longer pleased. The memories are fresh, the
product satisfying. In 1820, at seventy-seven
years of age, Thomas Jefferson removed the six
testaments from his shelf, where they had been
sitting for a decade and a half, and carved out
a Gospel for himself, one whose witness he
could respect and whose message he could
understand.

Thomas Jefferson's interest in the Bible was
restricted entirely to the life and teachings of
Jesus. Eloquent, benevolent, innocent, a victim
first of the Roman state and then of the Christian church, Jesus was the lamb whom human-
kind would never tire of slaughtering. In a
statement of his faith, Jefferson wrote to Rush,
"I am a Christian, in the only sense he wished
any one to be; sincerely attached to his doctrines, in preference to all others; ascribing to
himself every human excellence; and believing
he never claimed any other." Historian Daniel

J. Boorstin notes, "The Jeffersonian had projected his own qualities and limitations into Jesus, whose career became his vivid symbol of the superfluity and perils of speculative philosophy."

As with many Unitarians of like spirit who have followed him, Jefferson's was a search not so much for the historical as for the intelligible Jesus. John Adams recognized it as such in 1813 when he wrote to Jefferson, "I admire your employment in selecting the philosophy and divinity of Jesus, and separating it from all mixtures. If I had eyes and nerves I would go through both Testaments and mark all that I understand." Which is precisely what Thomas Jefferson did, not once but twice, with the Gospels.

The

Life and Morals

of

Jesus of Nazareth

Extracted textually

from the Gospels

in

Greek, Latin

French & English.

28 Καὶ προσελθὼν εἷς τῶν
γραμματέων, ἀκούσας αὐτῶν συ-
ζητούντων, εἰδὼς ὅτι καλῶς αὐ-
τοῖς ἀπεκρίθη, ἐπηρώτησεν αὐτὸν·
Ποία ἐστὶ πρώτη πασῶν ἐντολή;

29 Ὁ δὲ Ἰησοῦς ἀπεκρίθη αὐ-
τῷ· Ὅτι πρώτη πασῶν τῶν ἐν-
τολῶν· Ἄκουε Ἰσραήλ, Κύριος
ὁ Θεὸς ἡμῶν, Κύριος εἷς ἐστι·

30 Καὶ ἀγαπήσεις Κύριον τὸν
Θεόν σου ἐξ ὅλης τῆς καρδίας σου,
καὶ ἐξ ὅλης τῆς ψυχῆς σου, καὶ ἐξ
ὅλης τῆς διανοίας σου, καὶ ἐξ ὅλης
τῆς ἰσχύος σου· αὕτη πρώτη
ἐντολή.

31 Καὶ δευτέρα ὁμοία αὕτη·
Ἀγαπήσεις τὸν πλησίον σου ὡς
σεαυτόν· μείζων τούτων ἄλλη
ἐντολὴ οὐκ ἔστι.

40 Ἐν ταύταις ταῖς δυσὶν ἐν-
τολαῖς ὅλος ὁ νόμος καὶ οἱ προφῆται
κρέμανται.

32 Καὶ εἶπεν αὐτῷ ὁ γραμ-
ματεὺς· Καλῶς, διδάσκαλε, ἐπ᾽
ἀληθείας εἶπας ὅτι εἷς ἐστι Θεός,
καὶ οὐκ ἔστιν ἄλλος πλὴν αὐτοῦ·

33 Καὶ τὸ ἀγαπᾶν αὐτὸν ἐξ
ὅλης τῆς καρδίας, καὶ ἐξ ὅλης τῆς
συνέσεως, καὶ ἐξ ὅλης τῆς ψυχῆς,
καὶ ἐξ ὅλης τῆς ἰσχύος, καὶ τὸ
ἀγαπᾶν τὸν πλησίον ὡς ἑαυτόν,
πλεῖόν ἐστι πάντων τῶν ὁλοκαυ-
τωμάτων καὶ τῶν θυσιῶν.

Κεφ. κγ'. 23.

1 Τότε ὁ Ἰησοῦς ἐλάλησε τοῖς
ὄχλοις καὶ τοῖς μαθηταῖς

2 λέγων· Ἐπὶ τῆς Μωσέως
καθέδρας ἐκάθισαν οἱ Γραμματεῖς
καὶ οἱ Φαρισαῖοι·

3 Πάντα οὖν ὅσα ἂν εἴπωσιν
ὑμῖν τηρεῖν, τηρεῖτε καὶ ποιεῖτε·
κατὰ δὲ τὰ ἔργα αὐτῶν μὴ ποι-
εῖτε· λέγουσι γὰρ, καὶ οὐ ποιοῦσι.

4 Δεσμεύουσι γὰρ φορτία βαρέα
καὶ δυσβάστακτα, καὶ ἐπιτιθέασιν ἐπὶ
τοὺς ὤμους τῶν ἀνθρώπων· τῷ δὲ
δακτύλῳ αὐτῶν οὐ θέλουσι κινῆσαι
αὐτά·

* 5 Πάντα δὲ τὰ ἔργα αὐτῶν
ποιοῦσι πρὸς τὸ θεαθῆναι τοῖς
ἀνθρώποις· ‡ πλατύνουσι δὲ τὰ
† φυλακτήρια αὐτῶν, καὶ μεγαλύ-
νουσι τὰ κράσπεδα τῶν ἱματίων
αὐτῶν·

* 6 ‡ φιλοῦσι ‡ τε τὴν ‡ πρω-
τοκλισίαν ἐν τοῖς ‡ δείπνοις, καὶ
τὰς ‡ πρωτοκαθεδρίας ἐν ταῖς συν-
αγωγαῖς·

---

28 Et accedens unus Scri-
barum, audiens illos conqui-
rentes, videns quod pulchre illis
respondcrit, interrogavit eum:
quod esset primum omnium
mandatum?

29 At Jesus respondit ei, quia
primum omnium mandatorum:
Audi Israël, Dominus Deus no-
ster, Dominus unus est.

30 Et diliges Dominum Deum
tuum ex toto corde tuo, & ex
tota anima tua, & ex tota cogi-
tatione tua, & ex tota virtute
tua. Hoc primum mandatum.

31 Et secundum simile huic:
Diliges proximum tuum ut teip-
sum. Majus horum aliud mandatum non est.

40 In his duobus mandatis
universa Lex & Prophetæ pen-
dent.

32 Et ait illi Scriba: Pulchre
Magister in veritate dixisti, quia
unus est Deus, & non est alius
præter eum.

33 Et diligere eum ex toto
corde, & ex toto intellectu, &
ex tota anima, & ex tota forti-
tudine: & diligere proximum
ut seipsum, plus est omnibus
holocautomatibus, & sacrificiis.

CAPUT XXIII.

1 Tunc Jesus loquutus est
turbis, & discipulis

2 Dicens: Super Mosi ca-
thedram sederunt Scribæ &
Pharisæi:

3 Omnia ergo quæcumque
dixerint vobis servare, servate
& facite: secundùm verò opera
eorum ne facite: dicunt enim,
& non faciunt.

4 Alligant enim onera gravia
& importabilia, & imponunt in
humeros hominum: at digito
suo non volunt movere ea.

5 Omnia verò opera sua faciunt adspectari hominibus, di-
latant verò phylacteria sua, &
magnificant fimbrias vestimen-
torum suorum.

6 Amantque primos recubi-
tus in cœnis, & primas cathe-
dras in synagogis.

28. Alors un des Scribes, qui les avoit ouï disputer ensemble, voyant qu'il leur avoit bien répondu, s'approcha, et lui demanda : Quel est le premier de tous les commandemens?

29. Jésus lui répondit : Le premier de tous les commandemens *est celui-ci* : Ecoute Israël, le Seigneur notre Dieu est le seul Seigneur.

30. Tu aimeras le Seigneur ton Dieu, de tout ton cœur, de toute ton ame, de toute ta pensée, et de toute ta force. C'est là le premier commandement.

31. Et voici le second, *qui lui est semblable* : Tu aimeras ton prochain comme toi-même. Il n'y a point d'autre commandement, plus grand que ceux-ci.

40. Toute la loi et les Prophètes se rapportent à ces deux commandemens.

32. Et le Scribe lui répondit : Maître, tu as bien dit, et selon la vérité, qu'il n'y a qu'un seul Dieu, et qu'il n'y en a point d'autre que lui ;

33. Et que l'aimer de tout son cœur, de toute son intelligence, de toute *son* ame, et de toute sa force, et aimer *son* prochain comme soi-même, c'est plus que tous les holocaustes et que tous les sacrifices.

A tors Jésus parla au peuple, et à ses Disciples,

2. Et leur dit : Les Scribes et les Pharisiens sont assis sur la chaire de Moyse.

3. Observez donc, et faites tout ce qu'ils vous diront d'observer ; mais ne faites pas comme ils font ; parce qu'ils disent et ne font pas.

4. Car ils lient des fardeaux pesans et insupportables, et les mettent sur les épaules des hommes ; mais ils ne voudroient pas les remuer du doigt.

5. Et ils font toutes leurs actions, afin que les hommes les voient ; car ils portent de larges phylactères, et ils ont de plus longues franges à leurs habits ;

6. Ils aiment à avoir les premières places dans les festins, et les premiers sieges dans les Synagogues ;

28 And one of the scribes came, and having heard them reasoning together, and perceiving that he had answered them well, asked him, Which is the first commandment of all? *Mk. 12.*

29 And Jesus answered him, The first of all the commandments *is,* Hear, O Israel ; The Lord our God is one Lord :

30 And thou shalt love the Lord thy God with all thy heart, and with all thy soul, and with all thy mind, and with all thy strength. This *is* the first commandment.

31 And the second *is* like, *namely* this, Thou shalt love thy neighbour as thyself. There is none other commandment greater than these.

40 On these two commandments hang all the law and the prophets. *M. 22.*

32 And the scribe said unto him, *Mk. 12.* Well, Master, thou hast said the truth : for there is one God ; and there is none other but he :

33 And to love him with all the heart, and with all the understanding, and with all the soul, and with all the strength, and to love *his* neighbour as himself, is more than all whole burnt-offerings and sacrifices.

CHAP. XXIII. *M.*

The Pharisees exposed, &c.

THEN spake Jesus to the multitude, and to his disciples

2 Saying, The scribes and the Pharisees sit in Moses' seat :

3 All therefore whatsoever they bid you observe, *that* observe and do ; but do not ye after their works : for they say and do not.

4 For they bind heavy burdens and grievous to be borne, and lay *them* on mens' shoulders ; but they *themselves* will not move them with one of their fingers.

5 But all their works they do for to be seen of men : they make broad their phylacteries, and enlarge the borders of their garments.

6 And love the uppermost rooms at feasts, and the chief seats in the synagogues.

A Table

the Texts ~~of this~~ ~~extracting~~ from the Evangelists, employed ~~in~~ this Narrative, and of the order of their arrangement.

2. 1—7. Joseph & Mary go to Bethlehem, where Jesus is born

2. 39. he is circumcised & named & they return to Nazareth

2. 42—48. 51. 52. at 12. years of age he accompanies his parents to Jerusalem and returns.

1.2. Mt. 1. & Mt. 3. 4. 5. 6. John baptises in Jordan.

3. 13 Jesus is baptised. L. 3. 23. at 30. years of age.

2. 12—16. drives the traders out of the temple.

3. 22. Mt. 4. 12. Mk. 6. 17—28. he ~~goes~~ into Galilee on the death of John baptises but retires

Mt. 4. 21. 22. he teaches in the Synagogue.

12. 1—5. 9—12. Mk. 2. 27. Mt. 12. 14. 15. explains the Sabbath.

L. 6. 12—17. call of his disciples.

Mt. ... L. 6. 24. 25. 26. Mt. 5. 13—47. L. 6. 34. 35. 36. Mt. 6. 1.—34. 7. 1. 2.

L. 6. 20. Mt. 7. 3—20. 12. 35. 36. 37. 7. 24—29. the Sermon in the Mount

Mt. 8. 1. Mk. 6. 6. Mt. 11. 28. 29. 30. exhorts.

16. L. 7. 36—46. a woman anointeth him.

17. Mk. 3. 31—35. L. 12. 1—7. 13—15. precepts

18. L. 12. 16.—21. parable of the rich man.

19. 22—48. 54. 59. precepts. L. 13. 1—5.

21. L. 13. 6—9. parable of the fig tree.

22. L. 14. 37—46. 52. 53. 54. precepts.

23. Mt. 13. 1—9. Mk. 4. 10. Mt. 13. 18—23. parable of the Sower.

25. Mk. 4. 21. 22. 23. precepts. Mt. 13. 24—30. 36—52. parable of the Tares.

27. Mk. 4. 26—34. L. 9. 57—62. L. 5. 27—29. Mk. 2. 15—17. precepts. L. 5. 36—39. parable of new wine in old bottles.

28. Mt. ... 53—57. a prophet hath no honor in his own country.

29. Mt. 9. 36. Mk. 6. 7. Mt. 10. 5. 6. 9—18. 23. 26—31. Mk. 6. 12. 30. mission, instruction, return

L. 7. 1. Mk. 7. 1—5. 14—24. Mt. 18. 1. 2. 7—9. 12—17. 21—22. precepts.

Mt. 18. 23.—35. parable of the wicked servant.

A TABLE of the Texts from the Evangelists employed in this Narrative and of the order of their arrangement.

*The numbers indicate the leaves in Jefferson's compilation. In the English text, as printed in this edition, they are shown in brackets on the inner margin.

[65] **Mt. 25.** 1-13. parable of the ten virgins.

[66]   14-30. parable of the talents.

[67, 68] **L. 21.** 34-36. **Mt. 25.** 31-46. the day of judgment.

[69] **Mk. 14.** 1-8. a woman anointeth him.

     Mt. 26. 14-16. Judas undertakes to point out Jesus.

[70, 71]   17-20. **L. 22.** 24-27. **J. 13.** 2. 4-17. 21-26. 31. 34. 35.

     Mt. 26. 31. 33.

[72] **L. 22.** 33-34. **Mt. 26.** 35-45. precepts to his disciples. washes their feet. trouble of mind and prayer.

[73] **J. 18.** 1-3. **Mt. 26.** 48-50. Judas conducts the officers to Jesus.

[74] **J. 18.** 4-8. **Mt. 26.** 50-52. 55. 56. **Mk. 14.** 51. 52. **Mt. 26.** 57. **J. 18.** 15. 16. 18. 17.

[75] **J. 18.** 25. 26. 27. **Mt. 26.** 75. **J. 18.** 19-23. **Mk. 14.** 55-61.

     L. 22. 67. 68. 70. **Mk. 14.** 63-65. he is arrested & carried before Caiaphas the High priest & is condemned.

[76] **J. 18.** 28-31. 33-38. **L. 23.** 5. **Mt. 27.** 13. is then carried to Pilate.

[77] **L. 23.** 6-12. who sends him to Herod.

[78] **L. 23.** 13-16. **Mt. 27.** 15-23. 26. receives him back, scourges and delivers him to execution.

[79, 80] **Mt. 27.** 27. 29-31. 3-8. **L. 23.** 26-32. **J. 19.** 17-24. **Mt. 27.** 39-43.

[81] **L. 23.** 39-41. 34. **J. 19.** 25-27. **Mt. 27.** 46-55. 56. his crucifixion. death and burial.

     J. 19. 31-34. 38-42. **Mt. 27.** 60. his burial.

36

THE LIFE AND MORALS OF
Jesus of Nazareth

[1] And it came to pass in those days, that there **L. 2/1**
went out a decree from Caesar Augustus,
that all the world should be taxed.

(And this taxing was first made when Cyrenius **2**
was governor of Syria.)

And all went to be taxed, every one into his **3**
own city.

And Joseph also went up from Galilee, out of **4**
the city of Nazareth, into Judaea unto the city
of David, which is called Bethlehem (because he
was of the house and lineage of David,)

To be taxed with Mary his espoused wife, being **5**
great with child.

And so it was, that, while they were there, the **6**
days were accomplished that she should be delivered

And s͏ ͏ brought forth her first-born son, and **7**
wrapped him in swaddling clothes, and laid him
in a manger; because there was no room for
them in the inn.

And when eight days were accomplished for the **21**
circumcising of the child, his name was called
JESUS,

37

L. 2/39 And when they had performed all things according to the law of the Lord, they returned into Galilee, to their own city Nazareth.

40 And the child grew, and waxed strong in spirit, filled with wisdom:

42 And when he was twelve years old, they went up to Jerusalem, after the custom of the feast.

43 And when they had fulfilled the days, as they returned, the child Jesus tarried behind in Jerusalem; and Joseph and his mother knew not of it.

44 But they, supposing him to have been in the company, went a day's journey; and they sought him among their kinsfolk and acquaintance.

45 And when they found him not, they turned back again to Jerusalem, seeking him.

46 And it came to pass, that after three days they [2] found him in the temple, sitting in the midst of the doctors, both hearing them, and asking them questions.

47 And all that heard him were astonished at his understanding and answers.

48 And when they saw him, they were amazed: and his mother said unto him, Son, why hast thou thus dealt with us? behold, thy father and I have sought thee sorrowing.

51 And he went down with them, and came to Nazareth, and was subject unto them:

52 And Jesus increased in wisdom and stature.

Now in the fifteenth year of the reign of **L. 3/1**
Tiberius Caesar, Pontius Pilate being
governor of Judaea, and Herod being
tetrarch of Galilee, and his brother Philip tetrarch of Ituraea and of the region of Tracho-
nitis, and Lysanias the tetrarch of Abilene,

Annas and Caiaphas being the high priests, **2**
John did baptize in the wilderness, **Mk. 1/4**
And the same John had his raiment of camel's **Mt. 3/4**
hair, and a leathern girdle about his loins; and
his meat was locusts and wild honey.

Then went out to him Jerusalem, and all Judaea, **5**
and all the region round about Jordan,

And were baptized of him in Jordan. **6**
Then cometh Jesus from Galilee to Jordan unto **Mt. 3/13**
John, to be baptized of him.

And Jesus himself began to be about thirty **L. 3/23**
years of age,

After this he went down to Capernaum, he, and **J. 2/12**
his mother, and his brethren, and his disciples:
and they continued there not many days.

[3] And the Jews' passover was at hand, and Jesus **13**
went up to Jerusalem,

And found in the temple those that sold oxen **14**
and sheep and doves, and the changers of money
sitting:

And when he had made a scourge of small **15**
cords, he drove them all out of the temple, and
the sheep and the oxen; and poured out the

J. 2/15 changers' money, and overthrew the tables;

16 And said unto them that sold doves, Take these things hence; make not my Father's house an house of merchandise.

J. 3/22 After these things came Jesus and his disciples into the land of Judaea; and there he tarried with them, and baptized.

Mt. 4/12 Now when Jesus had heard that John was cast into prison, he departed into Galilee;

Mk. 6/17 For Herod himself had sent forth and laid hold upon John, and bound him in prison for Herodias' sake, his brother Philip's wife: for he had married her.

18 For John had said unto Herod, It is not lawful for thee to have thy brother's wife.

19 Therefore Herodias had a quarrel against him, and would have killed him; but she could not:

20 For Herod feared John, knowing that he was a just man and an holy, and observed him; and when he heard him, he did many things, and heard him gladly.

21 And when a convenient day was come, that Herod on his birthday made a supper to his lords, high captains, and chief estates of Galilee;

22 And when the daughter of the said Herodias came in, and danced, and pleased Herod and them that sat with him, the king said unto the damsel, Ask of me whatsoever thou wilt and I will give it thee.

And he sware unto her, Whatsoever thou shalt ask of me, I will give it thee, unto half of my kingdom. **Mk. 6/23**

[4] And she went forth, and said unto her mother, What shall I ask? and she said, The head of John the Baptist. **24**

And she came in straightway with haste unto the king, and asked, saying, I will that thou give me, by and by in a charger, the head of John the Baptist. **25**

And the king was exceedingly sorry; yet for his oath's sake, and for their sakes which sat with him, he would not reject her. **26**

And immediately the king sent an executioner, and commanded his head to be brought: and he went and beheaded him in prison; **27**

And brought his head in a charger, and gave it to the damsel: and the damsel gave it to her mother. **28**

And they went into Capernaum; and straightway on the sabbath day he entered into the synagogue, and taught. **Mk. 1/21**

And they were astonished at his doctrine: for he taught them as one that had authority, and not as the scribes. **22**

At that time Jesus went on the sabbath day through the corn, and his disciples were an hungered, and began to pluck the ears of corn, and to eat. **Mt. 12/1**

Mt. 12/2 But when the Pharisees saw it, they said unto him, Behold, thy disciples do that which is not lawful to do upon the sabbath day.

3 But he said unto them, Have ye not read what David did, when he was an hungered, and they that were with him;

4 How he entered into the house of God, and did eat the shewbread, which was not lawful for him to eat, neither for them which were with him, but only for the priests?

5 Or have ye not read in the law, how that on the sabbath days the priests in the temple profane the sabbath, and are blameless?

9 And when he was departed thence, he went into [5] their synagogue:

10 And, behold, there was a man which had his hand withered. And they asked him, saying, Is it lawful to heal on the sabbath days? that they might accuse him.

11 And he said unto them, What man shall there be among you, that shall have one sheep, and if it fall into a pit on the sabbath day, will he not lay hold on it, and lift it out?

12 How much then is a man better than a sheep? Wherefore it is lawful to do well on the sabbath days.

Mk. 2/27 And he said unto them, The sabbath was made for man, and not man for the sabbath:

Mt. 12/14 Then the Pharisees went out, and held a council

against him, how they might destroy him.   **Mt. 12/14**

But when Jesus knew it, he withdrew himself **15**
from thence: and great multitudes followed him.

And it came to pass in those days that he went **L. 6/12**
out* into a mountain to pray, and continued all
night in prayer to God.

And when it was day, he called unto him his **13**
disciples: and of them he chose twelve, whom
also he named apostles;

Simon (whom he also named Peter), and Andrew **14**
his brother, James and John, Philip and Barthol-
omew,

Matthew and Thomas, James the son of Al- **15**
phaeus, and Simon called Zelotes,

And Judas the brother of James, and Judas Isca- **16**
riot, which also was the traitor.

And he came down with them, and stood in **17**
the plain, and the company of his disciples, and
a great multitude of people out of all Judaea
and Jerusalem, and from the sea coast of Tyre
and Sidon, which came to hear him,

[6]   And seeing the multitudes, he went up into **Mt. 5/1**
a mountain: and when he was set, his dis-
ciples came unto him:

And he opened his mouth, and taught them, **2**
saying,

Blessed are the poor in spirit: for theirs is the **3**
kingdom of heaven.

*Mr. Jefferson changed the word "out" to "up."

43

Mt. 5/4 Blessed are they that mourn: for they shall be comforted.

5 Blessed are the meek: for they shall inherit the earth.

6 Blessed are they which do hunger and thirst after righteousness: for they shall be filled.

7 Blessed are the merciful: for they shall obtain mercy.

8 Blessed are the pure in heart: for they shall see God.

9 Blessed are the peacemakers: for they shall be called the children of God.

10 Blessed are they which are persecuted for righteousness' sake: for theirs is the kingdom of heaven.

11 Blessed are ye when men shall revile you, and persecute you, and shall say all manner of evil against you falsely, for my sake.

12 Rejoice, and be exceeding glad: for great is your reward in heaven: for so persecuted they the prophets which were before you.

L. 6/24 But woe unto you that are rich! for ye have received your consolation.

25 Woe unto you that are full! for ye shall hunger. Woe unto you that laugh now! for ye shall mourn and weep.

26 Woe unto you, when all men shall speak well of you! for so did their fathers to the false prophets.

Ye are the salt of the earth: but if the salt have **Mt. 5/13**
lost his savour, wherewith shall it be salted? it
is thenceforth good for nothing, but to be cast
out, and to be trodden under foot of men.

Ye are the light of the world. A city that is set **14**
on an hill cannot be hid.

[7] Neither do men light a candle, and put it under **15**
a bushel, but on a candlestick; and it giveth
light unto all that are in the house.

Let your light so shine before men, that they **16**
may see your good works, and glorify your
Father which is in heaven.

Think not that I am come to destroy the law, **17**
or the prophets: I am not come to destroy, but
to fulfil.

For verily I say unto you, Till heaven and earth **18**
pass, one jot or one tittle shall in no wise pass
from the law, till all be fulfilled.

Whosoever therefore shall break one of these **19**
least commandments, and shall teach men so,
he shall be called the least in the kingdom of
heaven: but whosoever shall do and teach them,
the same shall be called great in the kingdom of
heaven.

For I say unto you, That except your right- **20**
eousness shall exceed the righteousness of the
scribes and Pharisees, ye shall in no case enter
into the kingdom of heaven.

Ye have heard that it was said by them of old **21**

45

Mt. 5/21   time, Thou shall not kill, and whosoever shall kill shall be in danger of the judgment:

22   But I say unto you, That whosoever is angry with his brother without a cause shall be in danger of the judgment: and whosoever shall say to his brother, Raca, shall be in danger of the council: but whosoever shall say, Thou fool, shall be in danger of hell fire.

23   Therefore if thou bring thy gift to the altar, and there rememberest that thy brother hath aught against thee;

24   Leave there thy gift before the altar, and go thy way; first be reconciled to thy brother, and then come and offer thy gift.

25   Agree with thine adversary quickly, whilst thou [8] are in the way with him; lest at any time the adversary deliver thee to the judge, and the judge deliver thee to the officer, and thou be cast into prison.

26   Verily I say unto thee, Thou shalt by no means come out thence, till thou hast paid the uttermost farthing.

27   Ye have heard that it was said by them of old time, Thou shalt not commit adultery:

28   But I say unto you, That whosoever looketh on a woman to lust after her hath committed adultery with her already in his heart.

29   And if thy right eye offend thee, pluck it out, and cast it from thee: for it is profitable for thee

that one of thy members should perish, and not **Mt. 5/29**
that thy whole body should be cast into hell.

And if thy right hand offend thee, cut it off, 30
and cast it from thee: for it is profitable for thee
that one of thy members should perish, and not
that thy whole body should be cast into hell.

It hath been said, Whosoever shall put away his 31
wife, let him give her a writing of divorcement:

But I say unto you, That whosoever shall put 32
away his wife, saving for the cause of fornication, causeth her to commit adultery: and
whosoever shall marry her that is divorced committeth adultery.

Again, ye have heard that it hath been said 33
by them of old time, Thou shalt not forswear
thyself, but shalt perform unto the Lord thine
oaths:

But I say unto you, Swear not at all; neither 34
by heaven; for it is God's throne:

[9] Nor by the earth; for it is his footstool: neither 35
by Jerusalem; for it is the city of the great King.

Neither shalt thou swear by thy head, because 36
thou canst not make one hair white or black.

But let your communication be, Yea, yea; Nay, 37
nay; for whatsoever is more than these cometh
of evil.

Ye have heard that it hath been said, An eye 38
for an eye, and a tooth for a tooth:

But I say unto you, That ye resist not evil: but 39

47

Mt. 5/39 whosoever shall smite thee on thy right cheek, turn to him the other also.

40 And if any man will sue thee at the law, and take away thy coat, let him have thy cloak also.

41 And whosoever shall compel thee to go a mile, go with him twain.

42 Give to him that asketh thee, and from him that would borrow of thee turn not thou away.

43 Ye have heard that it hath been said, Thou shalt love thy neighbour, and hate thine enemy.

44 But I say unto you, Love your enemies, bless them that curse you, do good to them that hate you, and pray for them which despitefully use you, and persecute you;

45 That ye may be the children of your Father which is in heaven: for he maketh his sun to rise on the evil and on the good, and sendeth rain on the just and on the unjust.

46 For if ye love them which love you, what reward have ye? do not even the publicans the same?

47 And if ye salute your brethren only, what do you more than others? do not even the publicans so?

L. 6/34 And if ye lend to them of whom ye hope to [10] receive, what thank have ye? for sinners also lend to sinners, to receive as much again.

35 But love ye your enemies, and do good, and lend, hoping for nothing again; and your reward shall be great, and ye shall be the children

of the Highest: for he is kind unto the unthank- L. 6/35
ful and to the evil.

Be ye therefore merciful, as your Father also is 36
merciful.

Take heed that ye do not your alms before Mt. 6/1
men, to be seen of them: otherwise ye
have no reward of your Father which is
in heaven.

Therefore when thou doest thine alms, do not 2
sound a trumpet before thee, as the hypocrites
do in the synagogues and in the streets, that
they may have glory of men. Verily I say unto
you, They have their reward.

But when thou doest alms, let not thy left hand 3
know what thy right hand doeth:

That thine alms may be in secret: and thy 4
Father which seeth in secret himself shall reward thee openly.

And when thou prayest, thou shalt not be as 5
the hypocrites are: for they love to pray standing in the synagogues and in the corners of the
streets, that they may be seen of men. Verily I
say unto you, They have their reward.

But thou, when thou prayest, enter into thy 6
closet, and when thou hast shut thy door, pray
to thy Father which is in secret; and thy Father
which seeth in secret shall reward thee openly.

But when ye pray, use not vain repetitions as 7
the heathen do: for they think that they shall

49

Mt. 6/7 be heard for their much speaking.

8 Be not ye therefore like unto them: for your Father knoweth what things ye have need of, before ye ask him.

9 After this manner therefore pray ye: Our Father [11] which art in heaven, Hallowed be thy name.

10 Thy kingdom come. Thy will be done in earth, as it is in heaven.

11 Give us this day our daily bread.

12 And forgive us our debts, as we forgive our debtors.

13 And lead us not into temptation, but deliver us from evil: For thine is the kingdom, and the power, and the glory, for ever. Amen.

14 For if ye forgive men their trespasses, your heavenly Father will also forgive you:

15 But if ye forgive not men their trespasses, neither will your Father forgive your trespasses.

16 Moreover, when ye fast, be not, as the hypocrites, of a sad countenance: for they disfigure their faces, that they may appear unto men to fast. Verily I say unto you, They have their reward.

17 But thou, when thou fastest, anoint thine head, and wash thy face;

18 That thou appear not unto men to fast, but unto thy Father which is in secret: and thy Father, which seeth in secret, shall reward thee openly.

19 Lay not up for yourselves treasures upon earth,

where moth and rust doth corrupt, and where **Mt. 6/19**
thieves break through and steal:

But lay up for yourselves treasures in heaven, **20**
where neither moth nor rust doth corrupt, and
where thieves do not break through nor steal:

For where your treasure is, there will your heart **21**
be also.

The light of the body is the eye: if therefore **22**
thine eye be single, thy whole body shall be full
of light.

[12] But if thine eye be evil, thy whole body shall **23**
be full of darkness. If therefore the light that is
in thee be darkness, how great is that darkness!

No man can serve two masters: for either he **24**
will hate the one, and love the other; or else he
will hold to the one, and despise the other. Ye
cannot serve God and mammon.

Therefore I say unto you, Take no thought for **25**
your life, what ye shall eat, or what ye shall
drink; nor yet for your body, what ye shall put
on. Is not the life more than meat, and the body
than raiment?

Behold the fowls of the air: for they sow not, **26**
neither do they reap, nor gather into barns; yet
your heavenly Father feedeth them. Are ye not
much better than they?

Which of you by taking thought can add one **27**
cubit unto his stature?

And why take ye thought for raiment? Con- **28**

Mt. 6/28 sider the lilies of the field, how they grow; they toil not, neither do they spin:

29 And yet I say unto you, That even Solomon in all his glory was not arrayed like one of these.

30 Wherefore, if God so clothe the grass of the field, which today is, and tomorrow is cast into the oven, shall he not much more clothe you, O ye of little faith?

31 Therefore, take no thought, saying, What shall we eat? or, What shall we drink? or, Wherewithal shall we be clothed?

32 (For after all these things do the Gentiles seek:) for your heavenly Father knoweth that ye have need of all these things.

33 But seek ye first the kingdom of God, and his righteousness; and all these things shall be added unto you.

34 Take therefore no thought for the morrow: for the morrow shall take thought for the things of itself. Sufficient unto the day is the evil thereof.

Mt. 7/1 Judge not, that ye be not judged. [13]

2 For with what judgment ye judge, ye shall be judged: and with what measure ye mete, it shall be measured to you again.

L. 6/38 Give, and it shall be given unto you; good measure, pressed down, and shaken together, and running over, shall men give into your bosom.

52

And why beholdest thou the mote that is in thy **Mt. 7/3**
brother's eye, but considerest not the beam
that is in thine own eye?

Or how wilt thou say to thy brother, Let me **4**
pull out the mote out of thine eye; and, behold,
a beam is in thine own eye?

Thou hypocrite, first cast out the beam out of **5**
thine own eye; and then shalt thou see clearly
to cast out the mote out of thy brother's eye.

Give not that which is holy unto the dogs, **6**
neither cast ye your pearls before swine, lest
they trample them under their feet, and turn
again and rend you.

Ask, and it shall be given you; seek, and ye **7**
shall find; knock, and it shall be opened unto
you:

For every one that asketh receiveth; and he **8**
that seeketh findeth; and to him that knocketh
it shall be opened.

Or what man is there of you, whom if his son **9**
ask bread, will he give him a stone?

Or if he ask a fish, will he give him a serpent? **10**

If ye then, being evil, know how to give good **11**
gifts unto your children, how much more shall
your Father, which is in heaven, give good
things to them that ask him?

Therefore all things whatsoever ye would that **12**
men should do to you, do ye even so to them:
for this is the law and the prophets.

53

Mt. 7/13 Enter ye in at the strait gate: for wide is the [14]
gate, and broad is the way, that leadeth to de-
struction, and many there be which go in there-
at:

14 Because strait is the gate, and narrow is the
way, which leadeth unto life, and few there be
that find it.

15 Beware of false prophets, which come to you in
sheep's clothing, but inwardly they are ravening wolves.

16 Ye shall know them by their fruits. Do men
gather grapes of thorns, or figs of thistles?

17 Even so every good tree bringeth forth good
fruit; but a corrupt tree bringeth forth evil
fruit.

18 A good tree cannot bring forth evil fruit,
neither can a corrupt tree bring forth good
fruit.

19 Every tree that bringeth not forth good fruit
is hewn down, and cast into the fire.

20 Wherefore by their fruits ye shall know them.

Mt. 12/35 A good man out of the good treasure of the
heart bringeth forth good things: and an evil
man out of the evil treasure bringeth forth evil
things.

36 But I say unto you, That every idle word that
men shall speak, they shall give account thereof
in the day of judgment.

37 For by thy words thou shalt be justified, and by

thy words thou shalt be condemned. **Mt. 12/37**

Therefore whosoever heareth these sayings of **Mt. 7/24**
mine, and doeth them, I will liken him unto a
wise man, which built his house upon a rock:

And the rain descended, and the floods came, **25**
and the winds blew, and beat upon that house;
and it fell not; for it was founded upon a rock.

[15] And every one that heareth these sayings of **26**
mine, and doeth them not, shall be likened unto
a foolish man, which built his house upon the
sand:

And the rain descended, and the floods came, **27**
and the winds blew, and beat upon that house;
and it fell; and great was the fall of it.

And it came to pass, when Jesus had ended **28**
these sayings, the people were astonished at his
doctrine.

For he taught them as one having authority, **29**
and not as the scribes.

When he was come down from the moun- **Mt. 8/1**
tain, great multitudes followed him.
And he went round about the villages, **Mk. 6/6**
teaching.

Come unto me, all ye that labour and are heavy **Mt. 11/28**
laden, and I will give you rest.

Take my yoke upon you, and learn of me; for I **29**
am meek and lowly in heart: and ye shall find
rest unto your souls.

For my yoke is easy, and my burden is light. **30**

L. 7/36 And one of the Pharisees desired him that he would eat with him. And he went into the Pharisee's house, and sat down to meat.

37 And, behold, a woman in the city, which was a sinner, when she knew that Jesus sat at meat in the Pharisee's house, brought an alabaster box of ointment.

38 And stood at his feet behind him weeping, and began to wash his feet with tears, and did wipe them with the hairs of her head, and kissed his feet, and anointed them with the ointment.

39 Now when the Pharisee which had bidden him [16] saw it, he spake within himself, saying, This man, if he were a prophet, would have known who and what manner of woman this is that toucheth him: for she is a sinner.

40 And Jesus answering said unto him, Simon, I have somewhat to say unto thee. And he saith, Master, say on.

41 There was a certain creditor which had two debtors: the one owed five hundred pence, and the other fifty.

42 And when they had nothing to pay, he frankly forgave them both. Tell me therefore, which of them will love him most?

43 Simon answered and said, I suppose that he, to whom he forgave most. And he said unto him, Thou hast rightly judged.

44 And he turned to the woman, and said unto

56

Simon, Seest thou this woman? I entered into **L. 7/44** thine house, thou gavest me no water for my feet: but she hath washed my feet with tears, and wiped them with the hairs of her head.

Thou gavest me no kiss: but this woman since **45** the time I came in hath not ceased to kiss my feet.

My head with oil thou didst not anoint: but **46** this woman hath anointed my feet with ointment.

There came then his brethren and his mother, **Mk. 3/31** and, standing without, sent unto him, calling him.

And the multitude sat about him, and they said **32** unto him, Behold, thy mother and thy brethren without seek for thee.

And he answered them, saying, Who is my **33** mother, or my brethren?

And he looked round about on them which sat **34** about him, and said, Behold my mother and my brethren!

For whosoever shall do the will of God, the **35** same is my brother, and my sister, and mother.

[17] In the mean time, when there were gathered **L. 12/1** together an innumerable multitude of people, insomuch that they trode one upon another, he began to say unto his disciples first of all, Beware ye of the leaven of the Pharisees, which is hypocrisy.

57

L. 12/2 For there is nothing covered, that shall not be revealed; neither hid, that shall not be known.

3 Therefore whatsoever ye have spoken in darkness shall be heard in the light; and that which ye have spoken in the ear in closets shall be proclaimed upon the housetops.

4 And I say unto you my friends, Be not afraid of them that kill the body, and after that have no more that they can do.

5 But I will forewarn you whom ye shall fear: Fear him, which after he hath killed hath power to cast into hell; yea, I say unto you, Fear him.

6 Are not five sparrows sold for two farthings, and not one of them is forgotten before God?

7 But even the very hairs of your head are all numbered. Fear not therefore: ye are of more value than many sparrows.

13 And one of the company said unto him, Master, speak to my brother, that he divide the inheritance with me.

14 And he said unto him, Man, who made me a judge or a divider over you?

15 And he said unto them, Take heed, and beware of covetousness: for a man's life consisteth not in the abundance of things which he possesseth.

16 And he spake a parable unto them, saying, The ground of a certain rich man brought forth plentifully:

17 And he thought within himself, saying, What [18]

shall I do, because I have no room where to be- L. 12/17
stow my fruits?

And he said, This will I do: I will pull down my 18
barns, and build greater; and there will I be-
stow all my fruits and my goods.

And I will say to my soul, Soul, thou hast much 19
goods laid up for many years; take thine ease,
eat, drink, and be merry.

But God said unto him, Thou fool, this night 20
thy soul shall be required of thee: then whose
shall those things be, which thou hast provided?

So is he that layeth up treasure for himself, and 21
is not rich toward God.

And he said unto his disciples, Therefore I say 22
unto you, Take no thought for your life, what
ye shall eat; neither for the body, what ye shall
put on.

The life is more than meat, and the body is 23
more than raiment.

Consider the ravens: for they neither sow nor 24
reap; which neither have storehouse nor barn;
and God feedeth them: how much more are ye
better than the fowls?

And which of you with taking thought can add 25
to his stature one cubit?

If ye then be not able to do that thing which 26
is least, why take ye thought for the rest?

Consider the lilies how they grow: they toil 27

L. 12/27 not, they spin not; and yet I say unto you, that Solomon in all his glory was not arrayed like one of these.

28 If then God so clothe the grass, which is today in the field, and tomorrow is cast into the oven; how much more will he clothe you, O ye of little faith?

29 And seek not ye what ye shall eat, or what ye shall drink, neither be ye of doubtful mind.

30 For all these things do the nations of the world seek after: and your Father knoweth that ye have need of these things.

31 But rather seek ye the kingdom of God; and all [19] these things shall be added unto you.

32 Fear not, little flock; for it is your Father's good pleasure to give you the kingdom.

33 Sell that ye have, and give alms; provide yourselves bags which wax not old, a treasure in the heavens that faileth not, where no thief approacheth, neither moth corrupteth.

34 For where your treasure is, there will your heart be also.

35 Let your loins be girded about, and your lights burning;

36 And ye yourselves like unto men that wait for their lord, when he will return from the wedding; that when he cometh and knocketh, they may open unto him immediately.

37 Blessed are those servants, whom the lord when

he cometh shall find watching: verily I say unto L. 12/37
you, that he shall gird himself, and make them
to sit down to meat, and will come forth and
serve them.

And if he shall come in the second watch, or 38
come in the third watch, and find them so,
blessed are those servants.

And this know, that if the goodman of the 39
house had known what hour the thief would
come, he would have watched, and not have
suffered his house to be broken through.

Be ye therefore ready also: for the Son of Man 40
cometh at an hour when ye think not.

Then Peter said unto him, Lord, speakest thou 41
this parable unto us, or even to all?

And the Lord said, Who then is that faithful 42
and wise steward, whom his lord shall make
ruler over his household, to give them their
portion of meat in due season?

Blessed is that servant, whom his lord when he 43
cometh shall find so doing.

[20] Of a truth I say unto you, that he will make 44
him ruler over all that he hath.

But, and if that servant say in his heart, My lord 45
delayeth his coming; and shall begin to beat
the menservants and maidens, and to eat and
drink, and to be drunken;

The lord of that servant will come in a day 46
when he looketh not for him, and at an hour

L. 12/46 when he is not aware, and will cut him in sunder,

47 And that servant, which knew his lord's will, and prepared not himself, neither did according to his will, shall be beaten with many stripes.

48 But he that knew not and did commit things worthy of stripes, shall be beaten with few stripes. For unto whomsoever much is given, of him shall be much required: and to whom men have committed much, of him they will ask the more.

54 And he said also to the people, When ye see a cloud rise out of the west, straightway ye say, There cometh a shower; and so it is.

55 And when ye see the south wind blow, ye say, There will be heat; and it cometh to pass.

56 Ye hypocrites! ye can discern the face of the sky and of the earth; but how is it that ye do not discern this time?

57 Yea, and why even of yourselves judge ye not what is right?

58 When thou goest with thine adversary to the magistrate, as thou art in the way, give diligence that thou mayest be delivered from him; lest he hale thee to the judge, and the judge deliver thee to the officer, and the officer cast thee into prison.

59 I tell thee, thou shalt not depart thence, till thou hast paid the very last mite.

[21]   There were present at that season some **L. 13/1**
that told him of the Galilaeans, whose
blood Pilate had mingled with their sacrifices.

And Jesus answering said unto them, Suppose **2**
ye that these Galilaeans were sinners above all
the Galilaeans, because they suffered such
things?

I tell you, Nay: but, except ye repent, ye shall **3**
all likewise perish.

Or those eighteen, upon whom the tower in **4**
Siloam fell, and slew them, think ye that they
were sinners above all men that dwelt in Jerusalem?

I tell you, Nay: but, except ye repent, ye shall **5**
all likewise perish.

He spake also this parable; A certain man had **6**
a fig tree planted in his vineyard; and he came
and sought fruit thereon, and found none.

Then he said unto the dresser of his vineyard, **7**
Behold, these three years I come seeking fruit
on this fig tree, and find none: cut it down; why
cumbereth it the ground?

And he answering said unto him, Lord, let it **8**
alone this year also, till I shall dig about it, and
dung it:

And if it bear fruit, well: and if not, then after **9**
that thou shalt cut it down.

And as he spake, a certain Pharisee besought **L. 11/37**

L. 11/37 him to dine with him: and he went in, and sat down to meat.

38 And when the Pharisee saw it, he marvelled that he had not first washed before dinner.

39 And the Lord said unto him, Now do ye Pharisees make clean the outside of the cup and the platter; but your inward part is full of ravening and wickedness.

40 Ye fools! did not he that made which is without make that which is within also?

41 But rather give alms of such things as ye have; and, behold, all things are clean unto you.

42 But woe unto you, Pharisees! for ye tithe mint [22] and rue and all manner of herbs, and pass over judgment and the love of God: these ought ye to have done, and not to leave the other undone.

43 Woe unto you, Pharisees! for ye love the uppermost seats in the synagogues, and greetings in the markets.

44 Woe unto you, scribes and Pharisees, hypocrites! for ye are as graves which appear not, and the men that walk over them are not aware of them.

45 Then answered one of the lawyers, and said unto him, Master, thus saying thou reproachest us also.

46 And he said, Woe unto you also, ye lawyers! for ye lade men with burdens grievous to be

borne, and ye yourselves touch not the burdens L. 11/46
with one of your fingers.

Woe unto you, lawyers! for ye have taken away 52
the key of knowledge: ye entered not in yourselves, and them that were entering in ye hin-
dered.

And as he said these things unto them, the 53
scribes and the Pharisees began to urge him
vehemently, and to provoke him to speak of
many things:

Laying wait for him, and seeking to catch some- 54
thing out of his mouth, that they might accuse
him.

The same day went Jesus out of the house, Mt. 13/1
and sat by the sea side.

And great multitudes were gathered to- 2
gether unto him, so that he went into a ship,
and sat; and the whole multitude stood on the
shore.

And he spake many things unto them in para- 3
bles, saying, Behold, a sower went forth to sow;

And when he sowed, some seeds fell by the way 4
side, and the fowls came and devoured them:

[23] Some fell upon stony places, where they had 5
not much earth: and forthwith they sprung up,
because they had no deepness of earth:

And when the sun was up, they were scorched; 6
and because they had not root, they withered
away.

65

Mt. 13/7 And some fell among thorns; and the thorns sprung up, and choked them:

8 But other fell into good ground, and brought forth fruit, some an hundredfold, some sixtyfold, some thirtyfold.

9 Who hath ears to hear, let him hear.

Mk. 4/10 And when he was alone, they that were about him with the twelve asked of him the parable.

Mt. 13/18 Hear ye therefore the parable of the sower.

19 When any one heareth the word of the kingdom, and understandeth it not, then cometh the wicked one, and catcheth away that which was sown in his heart. This is he which received seed by the way side.

20 But he that received the seed into stony places, the same is he that heareth the word, and anon with joy receiveth it;

21 Yet hath he not root in himself, but dureth for a while; for when tribulation or persecution ariseth because of the word, by and by he is offended.

22 He also that received seed among the thorns is he that heareth the word; and the care of this world, and the deceitfulness of riches, choke the word, and he becometh unfruitful.

23 But he that received seed into the good ground is he that heareth the word, and understandeth it; which also beareth fruit, and bringeth forth, some an hundredfold, some sixty, some thirty.

[24] And he said unto them, Is a candle brought to **Mk. 4/21** be put under a bushel, or under a bed? and not to be set on a candlestick?

For there is nothing hid, which shall not be **22** manifested; neither was anything kept secret, but that it should come abroad.

If any man have ears to hear, let him hear. **23**

Another parable put he forth unto them, say- **Mt. 13/24** ing, The kingdom of heaven is likened unto a man which sowed good seed in his field:

But while men slept, his enemy came and sowed **25** tares among the wheat, and went his way.

But when the blade was sprung up, and brought **26** forth fruit, then appeared the tares also.

So the servants of the householder came and **27** said unto him, Sir, didst not thou sow good seed in thy field? from whence then hath it tares?

He said unto them, An enemy hath done this. **28** The servants said unto him, Wilt thou then that we go and gather them up?

But he said, Nay; lest while ye gather up the **29** tares, ye root up also the wheat with them.

Let both grow together until the harvest: and **30** in the time of harvest I will say to the reapers, Gather ye together first the tares, and bind them in bundles to burn them: but gather the wheat into my barn.

Then Jesus sent the multitude away, and went **36** into the house: and his disciples came unto him,

Mt. 13/36 saying, Declare unto us the parable of the tares of the field.

37 He answered and said unto them, He that soweth the good seed is the Son of Man;

38 The field is the world; the good seed are the children of the kingdom; but the tares are the children of the wicked one;

39 The enemy that sowed them is the devil; the harvest is the end of the world; and the reapers are the angels. [25]

40 As therefore the tares are gathered and burned in the fire; so shall it be in the end of this world.

41 The Son of Man shall send forth his angels, and they shall gather out of his kingdom all things that offend, and them which do iniquity;

42 And shall cast them into a furnace of fire; there shall be wailing and gnashing of teeth.

43 Then shall the righteous shine forth as the sun in the kingdom of their Father. Who hath ears to hear, let him hear.

44 Again, the kingdom of heaven is like unto treasure hid in a field; the which when a man hath found, he hideth, and for joy thereof goeth and selleth all that he hath, and buyeth that field.

45 Again, the kingdom of heaven is like unto a merchant man, seeking goodly pearls:

46 Who, when he had found one pearl of great

price, went and sold all that he had, and bought **Mt. 13/46**
it.

Again, the kingdom of heaven is like unto a **47**
net, that was cast into the sea, and gathered of
every kind:

Which, when it was full, they drew to shore, **48**
and sat down, and gathered the good into vessels, but cast the bad away.

So shall it be at the end of the world: the angels **49**
shall come forth, and sever the wicked from
among the just,

And shall cast them into the furnace of fire; **50**
there shall be wailing and gnashing of teeth.

Jesus saith unto them, Have ye understood all **51**
these things? They say unto him, Yea, Lord.

Then said he unto them, Therefore every scribe **52**
which is instructed unto the kingdom of heaven
is like unto a man that is an householder, which
bringeth forth out of his treasure things new
and old.

[26] And he said, So is the kingdom of God, as if a **Mk. 4/26**
man should cast seed into the ground;

And should sleep, and rise night and day, and **27**
the seed should spring and grow up, he knoweth
not how.

For the earth bringeth forth fruit of herself; **28**
first the blade, then the ear, after that the full
corn in the ear.

But when the fruit is brought forth, immediate- **29**

Mk. 4/29 ly he putteth in the sickle, because the harvest is come.

30 And he said, Whereunto shall we liken the kingdom of God? or with what comparison shall we compare it?

31 It is like a grain of mustard seed, which, when it is sown in the earth, is less than all the seeds that be in the earth:

32 But when it is sown, it groweth up, and becometh greater than all herbs, and shooteth out great branches; so that the fowls of the air may lodge under the shadow of it.

33 And with many such parables spake he the word unto them, as they were able to hear it.

34 But without a parable spake he not unto them: and when they were alone, he expounded all things to his disciples.

L. 9/57 And it came to pass, that, as they went in the way, a certain man said unto him, Lord, I will follow thee whithersoever thou goest.

58 And Jesus said unto him, Foxes have holes, and birds of the air have nests; but the Son of Man hath not where to lay his head.

59 And he said unto another, Follow me. But he said, Lord, suffer me first to go and bury my father.

60 Jesus said unto him, Let the dead bury their dead: but go thou and preach the kingdom of God.

And another also said, Lord, I will follow thee; **L. 9/61**
but let me first go bid them farewell, which are
at home at my house.

And Jesus said unto him, No man, having put **62**
his hand to the plough, and looking back, is fit
for the kingdom of God.

[27] And after these things he went forth, and saw **L. 5/27**
a publican, named Levi, sitting at the receipt of
custom: and he said unto him, Follow me.

And he left all, rose up, and followed him. **28**

And Levi made him a great feast in his own **29**
house: and

Many publicans and sinners sat also together **Mk. 2/15**
with Jesus and his disciples: for there were
many, and they followed him.

And when the scribes and Pharisees saw him eat **16**
with publicans and sinners, they said unto his
disciples, How is it that he eateth and drinketh
with publicans and sinners?

When Jesus heard it, he saith unto them, They **17**
that are whole have no need of the physician,
but they that are sick: I came not to call the
righteous, but sinners to repentance.

And he spake also a parable unto them; No **L. 5/36**
man putteth a piece of a new garment upon an
old; if otherwise, then both the new maketh a
rent, and the piece that was taken out of the
new agreeth not with the old.

And no man putteth new wine into old bottles; **37**

L. 5/37 else the new wine will burst the bottles, and be spilled, and the bottles shall perish.

38 But new wine must be put into new bottles; and both are preserved.

Mt. 13/53 And it came to pass, that when Jesus had finished these parables, he departed thence.

54 And when he was come into his own country, he taught them in their synagogue, insomuch that they were astonished, and said, Whence hath this man this wisdom, and these mighty works?

55 Is not this the carpenter's son? is not his mother called Mary? and his brethren, James, and Joses, and Simon, and Judas?

56 And his sisters, are they not all with us? When then hath this man all these things?   [28]

57 And they were offended in him. But Jesus said unto them, A prophet is not without honour save in his own country, and in his own house.

Mt. 9/36 But when he saw the multitudes, he was moved with compassion on them, because they fainted, and were scattered abroad, as sheep having no shepherd.

Mk. 6/7 And he called unto him the twelve and began to send them forth by two and two,

Mt. 10/5 And commanded them, saying, Go not into the way of the Gentiles, and into any city of the Samaritans enter ye not:

6 But go rather to the lost sheep of the house of Israel.

72

Provide neither gold, nor silver, nor brass in your purses, **Mt. 10/9**

Nor scrip for your journey, neither two coats, **10** neither shoes, nor yet staves: for the workman is worthy of his meat.

And into whatsoever city or town ye shall **11** enter, enquire who in it is worthy; and there abide till ye go thence.

And when ye come into an house, salute it. **12**

And if the house be worthy, let your peace **13** come upon it: but if it be not worthy, let your peace return to you.

And whosoever shall not receive you, nor hear **14** your words, when ye depart out of that house or city, shake off the dust of your feet.

Verily I say unto you, it shall be more tolerable **15** for the land of Sodom and Gomorrha in the day of judgment, than for that city.

Behold, I send you forth as sheep in the midst **16** of wolves: be ye therefore wise as serpents, and harmless as doves.

But beware of men: for they will deliver you up **17** to the councils, and they will scourge you in [29] their synagogues;

And ye shall be brought before governors and **18** kings for my sake, for a testimony against them and the Gentiles.

But when they persecute you in this city, flee **23** ye into another:

73

Mt. 10/26 Fear them not therefore: for there is nothing covered, that shall not be revealed; and hid, that shall not be known.

27 What I tell you in darkness, that speak ye in light: and what ye hear in the ear, that preach ye upon the housetops.

28 And fear not them which kill the body, but are not able to kill the soul: but rather fear him which is able to destroy both soul and body in hell.

29 Are not two sparrows sold for a farthing? and one of them shall not fall on the ground without your Father.

30 But the very hairs of your head are all numbered.

31 Fear ye not therefore, ye are of more value than many sparrows.

Mk. 6/12 And they went out and preached that men should repent.

30 And the apostles gathered themselves together unto Jesus, and told him all things, both what they had done and what they had taught.

J. 7/1 After these things Jesus walked in Galilee: for he would not walk in Jewry, because the Jews sought to kill him.

Mk. 7/1 Then came together unto him the Pharisees, and certain of the scribes, which came from Jerusalem.

2 And when they saw some of his disciples eat

bread with defiled (that is to say, with un- **Mk. 7/2**
washen) hands, they found fault.

For the Pharisees, and all the Jews, except they **3**
wash their hands oft, eat not, holding the tradition of the elders.

[30] And when they come from the market, except **4**
they wash, they eat not. And many other
things there be, which they have received to
hold, as the washing of cups, and pots, and of
brasen vessels, and tables.

Then the Pharisees and scribes asked him, Why **5**
walk not thy disciples according to the tradition of the elders, but eat bread with unwashen
hands?

And when he had called all the people unto **14**
him he said unto them, Hearken unto me every
one of you, and understand:

There is nothing from without a man, that **15**
entering into him can defile him: but the things
which come out of him, those are they that defile the man.

If any man have ears to hear, let him hear. **16**

And when he was entered into the house from **17**
the people, his disciples asked him concerning
the parable.

And he saith unto them. Are ye so without **18**
understanding also? Do ye not perceive, that
whatsoever thing from without entereth into
the man, it cannot defile him;

75

Mk. 7/19 Because it entereth not into his heart, but into the belly, and goeth out into the draught, purging all meats?

20 And he said, That which cometh out of the man, that defileth the man.

21 For from within, out of the heart of men, proceed evil thoughts, adulteries, fornications, murders,

22 Thefts, covetousness, wickedness, deceit, lasciviousness, an evil eye, blasphemy, pride, foolishness:

23 All these evil things come from within, and defile the man.

24 And from thence he arose, and went into the borders of Tyre and Sidon, and entered into an house, and would have no man know it: but he could not be hid.

Mt. 18/1 At the same time came the disciples unto [31] Jesus, saying, Who is the greatest in the kingdom of heaven?

2 And Jesus called a little child unto him, and set him in the midst of them,

3 And said, Verily I say unto you, Except ye be converted, and become as little children, ye shall not enter into the kingdom of heaven.

4 Whosoever therefore shall humble himself as this little child, the same is greatest in the kingdom of heaven.

7 Woe unto the world because of offences! for it

must needs be that offences come; but woe to **Mt. 18/7**
that man by whom the offence cometh!

Wherefore if thy hand or thy foot offend thee, 8
cut them off, and cast them from thee: it is
better for thee to enter into life halt or maimed,
rather than having two hands or two feet to be
cast into everlasting fire.

And if thine eye offend thee, pluck it out, and 9
cast it from thee: it is better for thee to enter
into life with one eye, rather than having two
eyes to be cast into hell fire.

How think ye? if a man have an hundred sheep, 12
and one of them be gone astray, doth he not
leave the ninety and nine, and goeth into the
mountains, and seeketh that which is gone
astray?

And if so be that he find it, verily I say unto 13
you, he rejoiceth more of that sheep, than of
the ninety and nine which went not astray.

Even so it is not the will of your Father which 14
is in heaven, that one of these little ones should
perish.

Moreover if thy brother shall trespass against 15
thee, go and tell him his fault between thee
and him alone: if he shall hear thee, thou hast
[32] gained thy brother.

But if he will not hear thee, then take with thee 16
one or two more, that in the mouth of two or
three witnesses every word may be established.

77

Mt. 18/17 And if he shall neglect to hear them, tell it unto the church: but if he neglect to hear the church, let him be unto thee as an heathen man and a publican.

21 Then came Peter to him, and said, Lord, how oft shall my brother sin against me, and I forgive him? till seven times?

22 Jesus saith unto him, I say not unto thee, Until seven times: but, Until seventy times seven.

23 Therefore is the kingdom of heaven likened unto a certain king, which would take account of his servants.

24 And when he had begun to reckon, one was brought unto him, which owed him ten thousand talents.

25 But forasmuch as he had not to pay, his lord commanded him to be sold, and his wife, and children, and all that he had, and payment to be made.

26 The servant therefore fell down, and worshipped him, saying, Lord, have patience with me, and I will pay thee all.

27 Then the lord of that servant was moved with compassion, and loosed him, and forgave him the debt.

28 But the same servant went out, and found one of his fellowservants, which owed him an hundred pence: and he laid hands on him, and took him by the throat, saying, Pay me that thou owest.

And his fellowservant fell down at his feet, and **Mt. 18/29** besought him, saying, have patience with me, and I will pay thee all.

And he would not: but went and cast him into **30** prison, till he should pay the debt.

[33] So when his fellowservants saw what was done, **31** they were very sorry, and came and told unto their lord all that was done.

Then his lord, after that he had called him, said **32** unto him, O thou wicked servant, I forgave thee all that debt, because thou desiredst me: Shouldest not thou also have had compassion **33** on thy fellowservant, even as I had pity on thee?

And his lord was wroth, and delivered him to **34** the tormentors, till he should pay all that was due unto him.

So likewise shall my heavenly Father do also **35** unto you, if ye from your hearts forgive not every one his brother their trespasses.

After these things the Lord appointed other **L. 10/1** seventy also, and sent them two and two before his face into every city and place, whither he himself would come.

Therefore said he unto them, The harvest truly **2** is great, but the labourers are few: pray ye therefore the Lord of the harvest, that he would send forth labourers into his harvest.

Go your ways: behold, I send you forth as **3** lambs among wolves.

79

L. 10/4 Carry neither purse, nor scrip, nor shoes: and salute no man by the way.

5 And into whatsoever house ye enter, first say, Peace be to this house.

6 And if the son of peace be there, your peace shall rest upon it: if not, it shall turn to you again.

7 And in the same house remain, eating and drinking such things as they give: for the labourer is worthy of his hire. Go not from house to house.

8 And into whatsoever city ye enter, and they receive you, eat such things as are set before you:

10 But into whatsoever city ye enter, and they re- [34] ceive you not, go your ways out into the streets of the same, and say,

11 Even the very dust of your city, which cleaveth on us, we do wipe off against you: notwithstanding be ye sure of this, that the kingdom of God is come nigh unto you.

12 But I say unto you that it shall be more tolerable in that day for Sodom, than for that city.

J. 7/2 Now the Jews' feast of tabernacles was at hand.

3 His brethren therefore said unto him, Depart hence, and go into Judaea, that thy disciples also may see the works that thou doest.

4 For there is no man that doeth any thing in secret, and he himself seeketh to be known openly. If thou do these things, shew thyself to the world.

For neither did his brethren believe in him. J. 7/5

Then Jesus said unto them, My time is not yet 6 come: but your time is alway ready.

The world cannot hate you; but me it hateth, 7 because I testify of it, that the works thereof are evil.

Go ye up unto this feast: I go not up yet unto 8 this feast; for my time is not yet full come.

When he had said these words unto them, he 9 abode still in Galilee.

But when his brethren were gone up, then went 10 he also up unto the feast, not openly, but as it were in secret.

Then the Jews sought him at the feast, and said, 11 Where is he?

And there was much murmuring among the 12 people concerning him: for some said, He is a good man; others said, Nay; but he deceiveth the people.

Howbeit no man spake openly of him for fear 13 of the Jews.

Now about the midst of the feast Jesus went up 14 into the temple, and taught.

And the Jews marvelled, saying, How knoweth 15 this man letters, having never learned?

Jesus answered them, and said,   16

[35] Did not Moses give you the law, and yet none 19 of you keepeth the law? Why go ye about to kill me?

J. 7/20 The people answered and said, Thou hast a devil: who goeth about to kill thee?

21 Jesus answered and said unto them, I have done one work, and ye all marvel.

22 Moses therefore gave unto you circumcision, (not because it is of Moses but of the fathers,) and ye on the sabbath day circumcise a man.

23 If a man on the sabbath day receive circumcision, that the law of Moses should not be broken; are ye angry at me, because I have made a man every whit whole on the sabbath day?

24 Judge not according to the appearance, but judge righteous judgment.

25 Then said some of them of Jerusalem, Is not this he, whom they seek to kill?

26 But, lo, he speaketh boldly, and they say nothing unto him. Do the rulers know indeed that this is the very Christ?

32 The Pharisees heard that the people murmured such things concerning him; and the Pharisees and the chief priests sent officers to take him.

43 So there was a division among the people because of him.

44 And some of them would have taken him; but no man laid hands on him.

45 Then came the officers to the chief priests and Pharisees; and they said unto them, Why have ye not brought him?

82

The officers answered, Never man spake like **J. 7/46**
this man.

Then answered them the Pharisees, Are ye also **47**
deceived?

Have any of the rulers or of the Pharisees be- **48**
lieved on him?

But this people who knoweth not the law are **49**
cursed.

[36] Nicodemus saith unto them, (he that came to **50**
Jesus by night, being one of them,)

Doth our law judge any man, before it hear **51**
him, and know what he doeth?

They answered and said unto him, Art thou **52**
also of Galilee? Search, and look: for out of
Galilee ariseth no prophet.

And every man went unto his own house. **53**

Jesus went unto the mount of Olives. **J. 8/1**
And early in the morning he came again **2**
into the temple, and all the people came
unto him; and he sat down, and taught them.

And the scribes and Pharisees brought unto him **3**
a woman taken in adultery; and when they had
set her in the midst,

They say unto him, Master, this woman was **4**
taken in adultery, in the very act.

Now Moses in the law commanded us, that **5**
such should be stoned: but what sayest thou?

This they said, tempting him, that they might **6**
have to accuse him. But Jesus stooped down,

J. 8/6 and with his finger wrote on the ground, as though he heard them not.

7 So when they continued asking him, he lifted up himself, and said unto them, He that is without sin among you, let him first cast a stone at her.

8 And again he stooped down, and wrote on the ground.

9 And they which heard it, being convicted by their own conscience, went out one by one, beginning at the eldest, even unto the last: and Jesus was left alone, and the woman standing in the midst.

10 When Jesus had lifted up himself, and saw none but the woman, he said unto her, Woman, where are those thine accusers? hath no man condemned thee?

11 She said, No man, Lord. And Jesus said unto her, Neither do I condemn thee: go, and sin no more.

J. 9/1 And as Jesus passed by, he saw a man which [37] was blind from his birth.

2 And his disciples asked him, saying, Master, who did sin, this man, or his parents, that he was born blind?

3 Jesus answered, Neither hath this man sinned, nor his parents: but that the works of God should be made manifest in him.

J. 10/1 Verily, verily, I say unto you, He that entereth not by the door into the sheepfold, but climb-

eth up some other way, the same is a thief and J. 10/1
a robber.

But he that entereth in by the door is the shep- 2
herd of the sheep.

To him the porter openeth; and the sheep hear 3
his voice; and he calleth his own sheep by
name, and leadeth them out.

And when he putteth forth his own sheep, he 4
goeth before them, and his sheep follow him:
for they know his voice.

And a stranger will they not follow, but will 5
flee from him: for they know not the voice of
strangers.

I am the good shepherd: the good shepherd giv- 11
eth his life for the sheep.

But he that is an hireling, and not the shepherd, 12
whose own the sheep are not, seeth the wolf
coming, and leaveth the sheep, and fleeth: and
the wolf catcheth them, and scattereth the
sheep.

The hireling fleeth, because he is an hireling, 13
and careth not for the sheep.

I am the good shepherd, and know my sheep 14
and am known of mine.

And other sheep I have, which are not of this 16
fold: them also I must bring, and they shall hear
my voice; and there shall be one fold, and one
shepherd.

[38] And, behold, a certain lawyer stood up, and L. 10/25

L. 10/25 tempted him, saying, Master, what shall I do to inherit eternal life?

26 He said unto him, What is written in the law? how readest thou?

27 And he answering said, Thou shalt love the Lord thy God with all thy heart, and with all thy soul, and with all thy strength, and with all thy mind; and thy neighbour as thyself.

28 And he said unto him, Thou hast answered right: this do, and thou shalt live.

29 But he, willing to justify himself, said unto Jesus, And who is my neighbour?

30 And Jesus answering said, A certain man went down from Jerusalem to Jericho, and fell among thieves, which stripped him of his raiment, and wounded him, and departed, leaving him half dead.

31 And, by chance, there came down a certain priest that way: and when he saw him, he passed by on the other side.

32 And likewise a Levite, when he was at the place, came and looked on him, and passed by on the other side.

33 But a certain Samaritan, as he journeyed, came where he was: and when he saw him, he had compassion on him.

34 And went to him, and bound up his wounds, pouring in oil and wine, and set him on his own

beast, and brought him to an inn, and took care   L. 10/34
of him.

And on the morrow when he departed, he took   35
out two pence, and gave them to the host, and
said unto him, Take care of him; and whatsoever thou spendest more, when I come again,
I will repay thee.

Which now of these three, thinkest thou, was   36
neighbour unto him that fell among the thieves?

And he said, He that shewed mercy on him.   37
Then said Jesus unto him, Go, and do thou
likewise.

[39]   And it came to pass, that, as he was praying   L. 11/1
in a certain place, when he ceased, one of
his disciples said unto him, Lord, teach
us to pray, as John also taught his disciples.

And he said unto them, When ye pray, say, Our   2
Father which art in heaven, Hallowed by thy
name. Thy kingdom come. Thy will be done, as
in heaven, so in earth.

Give us day by day our daily bread.   3

And forgive us our sins; for we also forgive   4
every one that is indebted to us. And lead us
not into temptation; but deliver us from evil.

And he said unto them, Which of you shall   5
have a friend, and shall go unto him at midnight, and say unto him, Friend, lend me three
loaves;

L. 11/6 For a friend of mine in his journey is come to me, and I have nothing to set before him?

7 And he from within shall answer and say, Trouble me not; the door is now shut, and my children are with me in bed; I cannot rise and give thee.

8 I say unto you, Though he will not rise and give him, because he is his friend, yet because of his importunity he will rise and give him as many as he needeth.

9 And I say unto you, Ask, and it shall be given you; seek, and ye shall find; knock, and it shall be opened unto you.

10 For every one that asketh receiveth; and he that seeketh findeth; and to him that knocketh it shall be opened.

11 If a son shall ask bread of any of you that is a father, will he give him a stone? or if he ask a fish, will he for a fish give him a serpent?

12 Or if he shall ask an egg, will he offer him a scorpion?

13 If ye then, being evil, know how to give good [40] gifts unto your children: how much more shall your heavenly Father give the Holy Spirit to them that ask him?

L. 14/1 And it came to pass, as he went into the house of one of the chief Pharisees to eat bread on the sabbath day, that they watched him.

88

And, behold, there was a certain man before L. 14/2
him which had the dropsy.

And Jesus answering spake unto the lawyers 3
and Pharisees, saying, Is it lawful to heal on the
sabbath day?

And they held their peace. 4
And he saith unto them,

Which of you shall have an ass or an ox fallen 5
into a pit, and will not straightway pull him out
on the sabbath day?

And they could not answer him again to these 6
things.

And he put forth a parable to those which were 7
bidden, when he marked how they chose out
the chief rooms; saying unto them,

When thou art bidden of any man to a wedding, 8
sit not down in the highest room; lest a more
honourable man than thou be bidden of him;

And he that bade thee and him come and say 9
to thee, Give this man place; and thou begin
with shame to take the lowest room.

But when thou art bidden, go and sit down in 10
the lowest room; that when he that bade thee
cometh, he may say unto thee, Friend, go up
higher: then shalt thou have worship in the
presence of them that sit at meat with thee.

For whosoever exalteth himself shall be abased; 11
and he that humbleth himself shall be exalted.

Then said he also to him that bade him, When 12

L. 14/12 thou makest a dinner or a supper, call not thy friends, nor thy brethren, neither thy kinsmen, nor thy rich neighbours; lest they also bid thee again, and a recompense be made thee.

13 But when thou makest a feast, call the poor, the [41] maimed, the lame, the blind:

14 And thou shalt be blessed; for they cannot recompense thee: for thou shalt be recompensed at the resurrection of the just.

16 Then said he unto him, A certain man made a great supper, and bade many:

17 And sent his servant at supper time to say to them that were bidden, Come; for all things are now ready.

18 And they all with one consent began to make excuse. The first said unto him, I have bought a piece of ground, and I must needs go and see it: I pray thee have me excused.

19 And another said, I have bought five yoke of oxen, and I go to prove them: I pray thee have me excused.

20 And another said, I have married a wife, and therefore I cannot come.

21 So that servant came, and shewed his lord these things. Then the master of the house being angry said to his servant, Go out quickly into the streets and lanes of the city, and bring in hither the poor, and the maimed, and the halt, and the blind.

And the servant said, Lord, it is done as thou L. 14/22
hast commanded, and yet there is room.

And the lord said unto the servant, Go out into 23
the highways and hedges and compel them to
come in, that my house may be filled.

For I say unto you, That none of those men 24
which were bidden shall taste of my supper.

For which of you, intending to build a tower, 28
sitteth not down first, and counteth the cost,
whether he have sufficient to finish it?

Lest haply, after he hath laid the foundation, 29
and is not able to finish it, all that behold it begin to mock him,

[42] Saying, This man began to build, and was not 30
able to finish.

Or what king, going to make war against an- 31
other king, sitteth not down first, and consult-
eth whether he be able with ten thousand to
meet him that cometh against him with twenty
thousand?

Or else, while the other is yet a great way off, 32
he sendeth an ambassage, and desireth condi-
tions of peace.

Then drew near unto him all the publicans L. 15/1
and sinners for to hear him.

And the Pharisees and scribes murmured, 2
saying, This man receiveth sinners, and eateth
with them.

And he spake this parable unto them saying, 3

91

L. 15/4 What man of you, having an hundred sheep, if he lose one of them, doth not leave the ninety and nine in the wilderness, and go after that which is lost, until he find it?

5 And when he hath found it, he layeth it on his shoulders, rejoicing.

6 And when he cometh home, he calleth together his friends and neighbours, saying unto them, Rejoice with me; for I have found my sheep which was lost.

7 I say unto you, that likewise joy shall be in heaven over one sinner that repenteth, more than over ninety and nine just persons, which need no repentance.

8 Either what woman having ten pieces of silver, if she lose one piece, doth not light a candle, and sweep the house, and seek diligently till she find it?

9 And when she hath found it, she calleth her friends and her neighbours together; saying, Rejoice with me; for I have found the piece which I had lost.

10 Likewise, I say unto you, there is joy in the presence of the angels of God over one sinner that repenteth.

11 And he said, A certain man had two sons: [43]

12 And the younger of them said to his father, Father, give me the portion of goods that falleth to me. And he divided unto them his living.

And not many days after the younger son gath- L. 15/13
ered all together, and took his journey into a
far country, and there wasted his substance
with riotous living.

And when he had spent all, there arose a mighty 14
famine in that land; and he began to be in want.

And he went and joined himself to a citizen of 15
that country; and he sent him into his fields to
feed swine.

And he would fain have filled his belly with the 16
husks that the swine did eat; and no man gave
unto him.

And when he came to himself, he said, How 17
many hired servants of my father's have bread
enough and to spare, and I perish with hunger!

I will arise and go to my father, and will say 18
unto him, Father, I have sinned against heaven,
and before thee,

And am no more worthy to be called thy son: 19
make me as one of thy hired servants.

And he arose, and came to his father. But when 20
he was yet a great way off, his father saw him,
and had compassion, and ran, and fell on his
neck, and kissed him.

And the son said unto him, Father, I have 21
sinned against heaven, and in thy sight, and am
no more worthy to be called thy son.

But the father said to his servants, Bring forth 22
the best robe, and put it on him; and put a ring

93

L. 15/22 on his hand, and shoes on his feet:

23 And bring hither the fatted calf, and kill it; and let us eat, and be merry:

24 For this my son was dead, and is alive again; he [44] was lost, and is found. And they began to be merry:

25 Now his elder son was in the field: and as he came and drew nigh to the house, he heard musick and dancing.

26 And he called one of the servants, and asked what these things meant.

27 And he said unto him, Thy brother is come; and thy father hath killed the fatted calf, because he hath received him safe and sound.

28 And he was angry, and would not go in: therefore came his father out, and entreated him.

29 And he answering said to his father, Lo, these many years do I serve thee, neither transgressed I at any time thy commandment: and yet thou never gavest me a kid, that I might make merry with my friends:

30 But as soon as this thy son was come, which hath devoured thy living with harlots, thou hast killed for him the fatted calf.

31 And he said unto him, Son, thou art ever with me, and all that I have is thine.

32 It was meet that we should make merry, and be glad; for this thy brother was dead, and is alive again; and was lost, and is found.

94

And he said also unto his disciples, There L. 16/1 was a certain rich man, which had a steward; and the same was accused unto him that he had wasted his goods.

And he called him, and said unto him, How is 2 it that I hear this of thee? give an account of thy stewardship; for thou mayest be no longer steward.

Then the steward said within himself, What 3 shall I do? for my lord taketh away from me the stewardship: I cannot dig; to beg I am ashamed.

[45] I am resolved what to do, that, when I am put 4 out of the stewardship, they may receive me into their houses.

So he called every one of his lord's debtors unto 5 him, and said unto the first, How much owest thou unto my lord?

And he said, An hundred measures of oil. And 6 he said unto him, Take thy bill, and sit down quickly, and write fifty.

Then saith he to another, And how much owest 7 thou? And he said, An hundred measures of wheat. And he said unto him, Take thy bill, and write fourscore.

And the lord commended the unjust steward, 8 because he had done wisely: for the children of this world are in their generation wiser than the children of light.

And I say unto you, Make to yourselves friends 9

L. 16/9 of the mammon of unrighteousness; that, when ye fail, they may receive you into everlasting habitations.

10 He that is faithful in that which is least is faithful also in much: and he that is unjust in the least is unjust also in much.

11 If therefore ye have not been faithful in the unrighteous mammon, who will commit to your trust the true riches?

12 And if ye have not been faithful in that which is another man's, who shall give you that which is your own?

13 No servant can serve two masters: for either he will hate the one, and love the other; or else he will hold to the one, and despise the other. Ye cannot serve God and mammon.

14 And the Pharisees also, who were covetous, heard all these things: and they derided him.

15 And he said unto them, Ye are they which justify yourselves before men; but God knoweth your hearts: for that which is highly esteemed among men is abomination in the sight of God.

18 Whosoever putteth away his wife, and marrieth [46] another, committeth adultery: and whosoever marrieth her that is put away from her husband committeth adultery.

19 There was a certain rich man, which was clothed in purple and fine linen, and fared sumptuously every day:

96

And there was a certain beggar named Lazarus, L. 16/20
which was laid at his gate full of sores,

And desiring to be fed with the crumbs which 21
fell from the rich man's table: moreover the
dogs came and licked his sores.

And it came to pass, that the beggar died, and 22
was carried by the angels into Abraham's bosom: the rich man also died, and was buried;

And in hell he lifted up his eyes, being in tor- 23
ments, and seeth Abraham afar off, and Lazarus
in his bosom.

And he cried, and said, Father Abraham, have 24
mercy on me; and send Lazarus, that he may
dip the tip of his finger in water, and cool my
tongue; for I am tormented in this flame.

But Abraham said, Son, remember that thou in 25
thy lifetime receivedst thy good things, and
likewise Lazarus evil things: but now he is
comforted, and thou art tormented.

And beside all this, between us and you there is 26
a great gulf fixed: so that they which would
pass from hence to you cannot; neither can
they pass to us, that would come from thence.

Then he said, I pray thee therefore, father, that 27
thou wouldest send him to my father's house:

For I have five brethren; that he may testify 28
unto them, lest they also come into this place
of torment.

Abraham saith unto him, They have Moses and 29

L. 16/29 the prophets; let them hear them.

30 And he said, Nay, father Abraham: but if one [47] went unto them from the dead, they will repent.

31 And he said unto him, If they hear not Moses and the prophets, neither will they be persuaded, though one rose from the dead.

L. 17/1 Then said he unto the disciples, It is impossible but that offences will come: but woe unto him, through whom they come!

2 It were better for him that a millstone were hanged about his neck, and he cast into the sea, than that he should offend one of these little ones.

3 Take heed to yourselves: If thy brother trespass against thee, rebuke him; and if he repent, forgive him.

4 And if he trespass against thee seven times in a day, and seven times in a day turn again to thee, saying, I repent; thou shalt forgive him.

7 But which of you, having a servant plowing or feeding cattle, will say unto him by and by, when he is come from the field, Go and sit down to meat?

8 And will not rather say unto him, Make ready wherewith I may sup, and gird thyself, and serve me, till I have eaten and drunken; and afterward thou shalt eat and drink?

9 Doth he thank that servant because he did the

things that were commanded him? I trow not. **L. 17/9**
So likewise ye, when ye shall have done all **10**
these things which are commanded you, say,
We are unprofitable servants: we have done
that which was our duty to do.

And when he was demanded of the Pharisees, **20**
when the kingdom of God should come, he
answered them and said, The kingdom of God
cometh not with observation:

[48] And as it was in the days of Noe, so shall it be **26**
also in the days of the Son of Man.

They did eat, they drank, they married wives, **27**
they were given in marriage, until the day that
Noe entered into the ark, and the flood came,
and destroyed them all.

Likewise also, as it was in the days of Lot; they **28**
did eat, they drank, they bought, they sold,
they planted, they builded;

But the same day that Lot went out of Sodom **29**
it rained fire and brimstone from heaven, and
destroyed them all.

Even thus shall it be in the day when the Son **30**
of Man is revealed.

In that day, he which shall be upon the house- **31**
top, and his stuff in the house, let him not come
down to take it away: and he that is in the field,
let him likewise not return back.

Remember Lot's wife. **32**

Whosoever shall seek to save his life shall lose **33**

L. 17/33 it: and whosoever shall lose his life shall preserve it.

34 I tell you, in that night there shall be two men in one bed; the one shall be taken, and the other shall be left.

35 Two women shall be grinding together; the one shall be taken, and the other left.

37 Two men shall be in the field; the one shall be taken, and the other left.

L. 18/1 And he spake a parable unto them to this end, that men ought always to pray, and not to faint;

2 Saying, There was in a city a judge, which feared not God, neither regarded man:

3 And there was a widow in that city; and she came unto him, saying, Avenge me of mine adversary.

4 And he would not for a while: but afterward he [49] said within himself, Though I fear not God, nor regard man;

5 Yet because this widow troubleth me, I will avenge her, lest by her continual coming she weary me.

6 And the Lord said, Hear what the unjust judge saith.

7 And shall not God avenge his own elect, which cry day and night unto him, though he bear long with them?

8 I tell you that he will avenge them speedily.

Nevertheless when the Son of Man cometh, L. 18/8
shall he find faith on the earth?

And he spake this parable unto certain which 9
trusted in themselves, that they were righteous,
and despised others:

Two men went up into the temple to pray; the 10
one a Pharisee, and the other a publican.

The Pharisee stood and prayed thus with him- 11
self, God, I thank thee, that I am not as other
men are, extortioners, unjust, adulterers, or
even as this publican.

I fast twice in the week, I give tithes of all that 12
I possess.

And the publican, standing afar off, would not 13
lift up so much as his eyes unto heaven, but
smote upon his breast, saying, God be merciful
to me a sinner.

I tell you, this man went down to his house jus- 14
tified rather than the other; for every one that
exalteth himself shall be abased; and he that
humbleth himself shall be exalted.

Now   came to pass, as they went, that he L. 10/38
entered into a certain village: and a certain
woman, named Martha, received him into her
house.

And she had a sister called Mary, which also sat 39
at Jesus' feet, and heard his word.

[50] But Martha was cumbered about much serving, 40
and came to him, and said, Lord, dost thou not

L. 10/40 care that my sister hath left me to serve alone? bid her therefore that she help me.

41 And Jesus answered and said unto her, Martha, Martha, thou art careful and troubled about many things:

42 But one thing is needful: and Mary hath chosen that good part, which shall not be taken away from her.

Mt. 19/1 And it came to pass, that when Jesus had finished these sayings, he departed from Galilee, and came into the coasts of Judaea beyond Jordan.

2 And great multitudes followed him;

3 The Pharisees also came unto him, tempting him, and saying unto him, Is it lawful for a man to put away his wife for every cause?

4 And he answered and said unto them, Have ye not read, that he which made them at the beginning made them male and female,

5 And said, For this cause shall a man leave father and mother, and shall cleave to his wife: and they twain shall be one flesh?

6 Wherefore they are no more twain, but one flesh. What therefore God hath joined together, let not man put asunder.

7 They say unto him, Why did Moses then command to give a writing of divorcement, and to put her away?

8 He saith unto them, Moses, because of the hard-

ness of your hearts suffered you to put away your **Mt. 19/8**
wives: but from the beginning it was not so.

And I say unto you, Whosoever shall put away **9**
his wife, except it be for fornication, and shall
marry another, committeth adultery: and whoso
marrieth her which is put away doth commit
adultery.

His disciples say unto him, If the case of the **10**
man be so with his wife, it is not good to marry.

[51] But he said unto them, All men cannot receive **11**
this saying, save they to whom it is given.

For there are some eunuchs, which were so born **12**
from their*—of heaven's sake. He that is able to
receive it, let him receive it.

Then were there brought unto him little chil- **13**
dren, that he should put his hands on them, and
pray: and the disciples rebuked them.

But Jesus said, Suffer little children, and forbid **14**
them not, to come unto me: for of such is the
kingdom of heaven.

And he laid his hands on them, and departed **15**
thence.

And, behold, one came and said unto him, Good **16**

---

*Mr. Jefferson omitted from his English text the words:
"mother's womb; and there are some eunuchs, which were
made eunuchs of men; and there be eunuchs, which have
made themselves eunuchs for the kingdom..." Since the
passage is found in the parallel Greek, Latin and French
texts its omission here was doubtless due to inadvertence
which he did not take the trouble to correct.

Mt. 19/16 Master, what good thing shall I do, that I may have eternal life?

17 And he said unto him, Why callest thou me good? there is none good but one, that is God: but if thou wilt enter into life, keep the commandments.

18 He saith unto him, Which? Jesus said, Thou shalt do no murder, Thou shalt not commit adultery, Thou shalt not steal, Thou shalt not bear false witness,

19 Honour thy father and thy mother: and, Thou shalt love thy neighbour as thyself.

20 The young man saith unto him, All these things have I kept from my youth up: what lack I yet?

21 Jesus said unto him, If thou will be perfect, go and sell that thou hast and give to the poor, and thou shalt have treasure in heaven: and come and follow me.

22 But when the young man heard that saying, he went away sorrowful: for he had great possessions.

23 Then said Jesus unto his disciples, Verily I say unto you, That a rich man shall hardly enter into the kingdom of heaven.

24 And again I say unto you, It is easier for a camel to go through the eye of a needle, than for a rich man to enter into the kingdom of God.

25 When his disciples heard it, they were exceedingly amazed, saying, Who then can be saved? [52]

But Jesus beheld them, and said unto them, **Mt. 19/26** With men this is impossible; but with God all things are possible.

For the kingdom of heaven is like unto a man **Mt. 20/1** that is an householder, which went out early in the morning to hire labourers into his vineyard.

And when he had agreed with the labourers for **2** a penny a day, he sent them into his vineyard.

And he went out about the third hour, and saw **3** others standing idle in the marketplace.

And said unto them; Go ye also into the vine- **4** yard, and whatsoever is right I will give you. And they went their way.

Again he went out about the sixth and ninth **5** hour, and did likewise.

And about the eleventh hour he went out, and **6** found others standing idle, and said unto them, Why stand ye here all the day idle?

They say unto him, Because no man hath hired **7** us. He saith unto them, Go ye also into the vineyard; and whatsoever is right, that shall ye receive.

So when even was come, the lord of the vine- **8** yard saith unto his steward, Call the labourers, and give them their hire, beginning from the last unto the first.

And when they came that were hired about the **9** eleventh hour, they received every man a penny.

Mt. 20/10 But when the first came, they supposed that they should have received more; and they likewise received every man a penny.

11 And when they had received it, they murmured against the good man of the house,

12 Saying, these last have wrought but one hour, and thou hast made them equal unto us, which have borne the burden and heat of the day.

13 But he answered one of them and said, Friend, [53] I do thee no wrong: didst not thou agree with me for a penny?

14 Take that thine is, and go thy way: I will give unto this last even as unto thee.

15 Is it not lawful for me to do what I will with mine own? Is thine eye evil, because I am good?

16 So the last shall be first, and the first last: for many be called, but few chosen.

L. 19/1 And Jesus entered and passed through Jericho.

2 And, behold, there was a man named Zacchaeus, which was the chief among the publicans, and he was rich.

3 And he sought to see Jesus who he was; and could not for the press, because he was little of stature.

4 And he ran before, and climbed up into a sycamore tree to see him: for he was to pass that way.

5 And, when Jesus came to the place, he looked

up, and saw him, and said unto him, Zacchaeus, L. 19/5
make haste, and come down; for today I must
abide at thy house.

And he made haste, and came down, and re- 6
ceived him joyfully.

And when they saw it, they all murmured, say- 7
ing, That he was gone to be guest with a man
that is a sinner.

And Zacchaeus stood, and said unto the Lord; 8
Behold, Lord, the half of my goods I give to
the poor; and if I have taken anything from
any man by false accusation, I restore him four-
fold.

And Jesus said unto him, This day is salvation 9
come to this house, forsomuch as he also is a
son of Abraham.

For the Son of Man is come to seek and to save 10
that which was lost.

And, as they heard these things, he added, and 11
spake a parable, because he was nigh to Jeru-
[54] salem, and because they thought that the kingdom of God should immediately appear.

He said therefore, A certain nobleman went into 12
a far country to receive for himself a kingdom,
and to return.

And he called his ten servants, and delivered 13
them ten pounds, and said unto them, Occupy
till I come.

But his citizens hated him, and sent a message 14

L. 19/14 after him, saying, We will not have this man to reign over us.

15 And it came to pass, that when he was returned, having received the kingdom, then he commanded these servants to be called unto him, to whom he had given the money, that he might know how much every man had gained by trading.

16 Then came the first, saying, Lord, thy pound hath gained ten pounds.

17 And he said unto him, Well, thou good servant: because thou hast been faithful in a very little, have thou authority over ten cities.

18 And the second came, saying, Lord, thy pound hath gained five pounds.

19 And he said likewise to him, Be thou also over five cities.

20 And another came, saying, Lord, behold, here is thy pound, which I have kept laid up in a napkin:

21 For I feared thee, because thou art an austere man: thou takest up that thou layedst not down, and reapest that thou didst not sow.

22 And he saith unto him, Out of thine own mouth will I judge thee, thou wicked servant. Thou knewest that I was an austere man, taking up that I laid not down, and reaping that I did not sow:

23 Wherefore then gavest not thou my money into

the bank, that at my coming I might have re- L. 19/23
quired mine own with usury?

[55] And he said unto them that stood by, take from 24
him the pound, and give it to him that hath ten
pounds.

(And they said unto him, Lord, he hath ten 25
pounds.)

For I say unto you, That unto every one which 26
hath shall be given; and from him that hath
not, even that he hath shall be taken away from
him.

But those mine enemies, which would not that 27
I should reign over them, bring hither, and slay
them before me.

And when he had thus spoken, he went before, 28
ascending up to Jerusalem.

And when they drew nigh unto Jerusalem, Mt. 21/1
and were come to Bethphage, unto the
mount of Olives, then sent Jesus two
disciples,

Saying unto them, Go into the village over 2
against you, and straightway ye shall find an ass
tied, and a colt with her: loose them, and bring
them unto me.

And if any man say aught unto you, ye shall 3
say, The Lord hath need of them; and straightway he will send them.

And the disciples went, and did as Jesus com- 6
manded them,

Mt. 21/7 And brought the ass, and the colt, and put on them their clothes, and they set him thereon.

8 And a very great multitude spread their garments in the way; others cut down branches from the trees, and strawed them in the way.

10 And when he was come into Jerusalem, all the city was moved, saying, Who is this?

J. 12/19 The Pharisees therefore said among themselves, Perceive ye how ye prevail nothing? behold, the world is gone after him.

20 And there were certain Greeks among them that came up to worship at the feast:

21 The same came therefore to Philip, which was [56] of Bethsaida of Galilee, and desired him, saying, Sir, we would see Jesus.

22 Philip cometh and telleth Andrew: and again Andrew and Philip tell Jesus.

23 And Jesus answered them, saying,

24 Verily, verily, I say unto you, Except a corn of wheat fall into the ground and die, it abideth alone: but if it die, it bringeth forth much fruit.

Mt. 21/17 And he left them, and went out of the city into Bethany; and he lodged there.

Mk. 11/12 And on the morrow, when they were come from Bethany,

15 Jesus went into the temple, and began to cast out them that sold and bought in the temple, and overthrew the tables of the money-changers, and the seats of them that sold doves;

110

And would not suffer that any man should carry any vessel through the temple. **Mk. 11/16**

And he taught, saying unto them, Is it not written, My house shall be called of all nations the house of prayer? but ye have made it a den of thieves. **17**

And the scribes and chief priests heard it, and sought how they might destroy him: for they feared him, because all the people was astonished at his doctrine. **18**

And when even was come, he went out of the city. **19**

[And they come again to Jerusalem: and he was walking in the temple, there come to him the chief priests, and the scribes, and the elders,]* **27**

And he said unto them, But what think ye? A certain man had two sons; and he came to the first, and said, Son, go work today in my vineyard. **Mt. 21/28**

He answered and said, I will not: but afterward he repented, and went. **29**

And he came to the second, and said likewise. And he answered, and said, I go, sir: and went not. **30**

Whether of them twain did the will of his father? They say unto him, The first. Jesus saith **31**

---

*The text does not give this verse but that Mr. Jefferson intended to include it is indicated by his marginal note reading "+ Mark 11.27."

Mt. 21/31   unto them, Verily I say unto you, That the publicans and the harlots go into the kingdom of God before you.

33   Hear another parable: [57]

Mk. 12/1   A certain man planted a vineyard, and set an hedge about it, and digged a place for the winevat, and built a tower, and let it out to husbandmen, and went into a far country.

2   And at the season he sent to the husbandmen a servant, that he might receive from the husbandmen of the fruit of the vineyard.

3   And they caught him, and beat him, and sent him away empty.

4   And again he sent unto them another servant; and at him they cast stones, and wounded him in the head, and sent him away shamefully handled.

5   And again he sent another; and him they killed, and many others; beating some, and killing some.

6   Having yet therefore one son, his well-beloved, he sent him also last unto them, saying, They will reverence my son.

7   But those husbandmen said among themselves, This is the heir; come, let us kill him, and the inheritance shall be ours.

8   And they took him, and killed him, and cast him out of the vineyard.

112

What shall therefore the lord of the vineyard   Mk. 12/9
do? he will come and destroy the husbandmen,
and will give the vineyard unto others.

And when the chief priests and Pharisees had   Mt. 21/45
heard his parables, they perceived that he spake
of them.

But when they sought to lay hands on him, they   46
feared the multitude, because they took him for
a prophet.

And Jesus answered and spake unto them   Mt. 22/1
again by parables, and said,
The kingdom of heaven is like unto a   2
certain king, which made a marriage for his son.

And sent forth his servants to call them that   3
were bidden to the wedding: and they would
not come.

[58]   Again, he sent forth other servants, saying, Tell   4
them which are bidden, Behold, I have prepared
my dinner: my oxen and my fatlings are killed,
and all things are ready: come unto the marriage.

But they made light of it, and went their ways,   5
one to his farm, another to his merchandise:

And the remnant took his servants and in-   6
treated them spitefully, and slew them.

But when the king heard thereof, he was wroth: 7
and he sent forth his armies, and destroyed
those murderers, and burned up their city.

113

Mt. 22/8 Then saith he to his servants, The wedding is ready, but they which were bidden were not worthy.

9 Go ye therefore into the highways, and as many as ye shall find, bid to the marriage.

10 So those servants went out into the highways, and gathered together all as many as they found, both bad and good: and the wedding was furnished with guests.

11 And when the king came in to see the guests, he saw there a man which had not on a wedding garment:

12 And he saith unto him, Friend, how camest thou in hither not having a wedding garment? And he was speechless.

13 Then saith the king to the servants, Bind him hand and foot, and take him away, and cast him into outer darkness; there shall be weeping and gnashing of teeth.

14 For many are called, but few are chosen.

15 Then went the Pharisees, and took counsel how they might entangle him in his talk.

16 And they sent out unto him their disciples with the Herodians, saying, Master, we know that thou art true, and teachest the way of God in truth, neither carest thou for any man: for thou regardest not the person of men.

17 Tell us therefore, What thinkest thou? Is it lawful to give tribute unto Caesar, or not?

But Jesus perceived their wickedness, and said, **Mt. 22/18**
[59] Why tempt ye me, ye hypocrites?

Shew me the tribute-money. And they brought 19
unto him a penny.

And he saith unto them, Whose is this image 20
and superscription?

They say unto him, Caesar's. Then saith he 21
unto them, Render therefore unto Caesar the
things which are Caesar's; and unto God the
things that are God's.

When they had heard these words, they mar- 22
velled, and left him, and went their way.

The same day came to him the Sadducees, which 23
say that there is no resurrection, and asked him,

Saying, Master, Moses said, If a man die, having 24
no children, his brother shall marry his wife,
and raise up seed unto his brother.

Now, there were with us seven brethren: and the 25
first, when he had married a wife, deceased, and
having no issue, left his wife unto his brother:

Likewise the second also, and the third, unto 26
the seventh.

And last of all the woman died also. 27

Therefore, in the resurrection, whose wife shall
she be of the seven? for they all had her.

Jesus answered and said unto them, Ye do err, 29
not knowing the scriptures, nor the power of
God.

For in the resurrection they neither marry, nor 30

115

Mt. 22/30 are given in marriage; but are as the angels of God in heaven.

31 But as touching the resurrection of the dead, have ye not read that which was spoken unto you by God, saying,

32 I am the God of Abraham, and the God of Isaac, and the God of Jacob? God is not the God of the dead, but of the living.

33 And when the multitude heard this, they were astonished at his doctrine.

Mk. 12/28 And one of the scribes came, and having heard [60] them reasoning together, and perceiving that he had answered them well, asked him, Which is the first commandment of all?

29 And Jesus answered him, The first of all the commandments is, Hear, O Israel; The Lord our God is one Lord:

30 And thou shalt love the Lord thy God with all thy heart, and with all thy soul, and with all thy mind, and with all thy strength. This is the first commandment.

31 And the second is like, namely this, Thou shalt love thy neighbour as thyself. There is none other commandment greater than these.

Mt. 22/40 On these two commandments hang all the law and the prophets.

Mk. 12/32 And the scribe said unto him, Well, Master, thou hast said the truth: for there is one God; and there is none other but he:

116

And to love him with all the heart, and with all   Mk. 12/33
the understanding, and with all the soul, and
with all the strength, and to love his neighbour
as himself, is more than all whole burnt-offerings and sacrifices.

Then spake Jesus to the multitude, and to   Mt. 23/1
his disciples,
Saying, The scribes and the Pharisees sit 2
in Moses' seat:

All therefore whatsoever they bid you observe, 3
that observe and do; but do not ye after their
works: for they say, and do not.

For they bind heavy burdens and grievous to be 4
borne, and lay them on men's shoulders; but
they themselves will not move them with one
of their fingers.

But all their works they do for to be seen of 5
men: they make broad their phylacteries, and
enlarge the borders of their garments.

And love the uppermost rooms at feasts, and 6
the chief seats in the synagogues,

[61] And greetings in the markets, and to be called 7
of men, Rabbi, Rabbi.

But be not ye called Rabbi: for one is your 8
Master, even Christ; and all ye are brethren.

And call no man your father upon the earth: for 9
one is your Father, which is in heaven.

Neither be ye called masters: for one is your 10
Master, even Christ.

117

Mt. 23/11 But he that is greatest among you shall be your servant.

12 And whosoever shall exalt himself shall be abased; and he that shall humble himself shall be exalted.

13 But woe unto you, scribes and Pharisees, hypocrites! for ye shut up the kingdom of heaven against men: for ye neither go in yourselves, neither suffer ye them that are entering, to go in.

14 Woe unto you, scribes and Pharisees, hypocrites! for ye devour widows' houses, and for a pretence make long prayer: therefore ye shall receive the greater damnation.

15 Woe unto you, scribes and Pharisees, hypocrites! for ye compass sea and land to make one proselyte, and when he is made, ye make him twofold more the child of hell than yourselves.

16 Woe unto you, ye blind guides, which say, Whosoever shall swear by the temple, it is nothing; but whosoever shall swear by the gold of the temple, he is a debtor.

17 Ye fools and blind! for whether is greater, the gold, or the temple that sanctifieth the gold?

18 And, Whosoever shall swear by the altar, it is nothing; but whosoever sweareth by the gift that is upon it, he is guilty.

19 Ye fools and blind! for whether is greater, the gift, or the altar that sanctifieth the gift?

20 Whoso therefore shall swear by the altar, swear- [62]

118

eth by it, and by all things thereon.   Mt. 23/20

And whoso shall swear by the temple, sweareth 21 by it, and by him that dwelleth therein.

And he that shall swear by heaven, sweareth by 22 the throne of God, and by him that sitteth thereon.

Woe unto you, scribes and Pharisees, hypo- 23 crites! for ye pay tithe of mint, and anise, and cummin, and have omitted the weightier matters of the law, judgment, mercy, and faith: these ought ye to have done, and not to leave the other undone.

Ye blind guides! which strain at a gnat, and 24 swallow a camel.

Woe unto you, scribes and Pharisees, hypo- 25 crites! for ye make clean the outside of the cup and of the platter, but within they are full of extortion and excess.

Thou blind Pharisee, cleanse first that which is 26 within the cup and platter, that the outside of them may be clean also.

Woe unto you, scribes and Pharisees, hypo- 27 crites! for ye are like unto whited sepulchres, which indeed appear beautiful outward, but are within full of dead men's bones, and of all uncleanness.

Even so ye also outwardly appear righteous 28 unto men, but within ye are full of hypocrisy and iniquity.

Mt. 23/29 Woe unto you, scribes and Pharisees, hypocrites! because ye build the tombs of the prophets, and garnish the sepulchres of the righteous,

30 And say, If we had been in the days of our fathers, we would not have been partakers with them in the blood of the prophets.

31 Wherefore ye be witnesses unto yourselves, that ye are the children of them which killed the prophets.

32 Fill ye up then the measure of your fathers.

33 Ye serpents, ye generation of vipers! how can ye escape the damnation of hell?

Mk. 12/41 And Jesus sat over against the treasury, and beheld how the people cast money into the treasury: and many that were rich cast in much. [63]

42 And there came a certain poor widow, and she threw in two mites, which make a farthing.

43 And he called unto him his disciples, and saith unto them, Verily I say unto you, That this poor widow hath cast more in, than all they which have cast into the treasury:

44 For all they did cast in of their abundance; but she of her want did cast in all that she had, even all her living.

Mt. 24/1 And Jesus went out, and departed from the temple: and his disciples came to him for to shew him the buildings of the temple. And Jesus said unto them, See ye not all these things? verily I say unto you, There shall not be

left here one stone upon another, that shall not **Mt. 24/2**
be thrown down.

Then let them which be in Judaea flee into the **16**
mountains:

Let him which is on the housetop not come **17**
down to take any thing out of his house:

Neither let him which is in the field return back **18**
to take his clothes.

And woe unto them that are with child, and to **19**
them that give suck in those days!

But pray ye that your flight be not in the win- **20**
ter, neither on the sabbath day:

For then shall be great tribulations, such as was **21**
not since the beginning of the world to this
time, no, nor ever shall be.

Immediately after the tribulation of those days **29**
shall the sun be darkened, and the moon shall
not give her light, and the stars shall fall from
heaven, and the powers of the heavens shall be
shaken.

[64] Now learn a parable of the fig tree; When his **32**
branch is yet tender, and putteth forth leaves,
ye know that summer is nigh:

So likewise ye, when ye shall see all these **33**
things, know that it is near, even at the doors.

But of that day and hour knoweth no man, no, **36**
not the angels of heaven, but my Father only.

But as the days of Noe were so shall also the **37**
coming of the Son of Man be.

Mt. 24/38 For as in the days that were before the flood they were eating and drinking, marrying and giving in marriage, until the day that Noe entered into the ark,

39 And knew not until the flood came, and took them all away;

40 Then shall two be in the field; the one shall be taken, and the other left.

41 Two women shall be grinding at the mill; the one shall be taken and the other left.

42 Watch therefore: for ye know not what hour your Lord doth come.

43 But know this, that if the good man of the house had known in what watch the thief would come, he would have watched, and would not have suffered his house to be broken up.

44 Therefore be ye also ready:

45 Who then is a faithful and wise servant, whom his lord hath made ruler over his household, to give them meat in due season?

46 Blessed is that servant, whom his lord when he cometh shall find so doing.

47 Verily I say unto you, That he shall make him ruler over all his goods.

48 But and if that evil servant shall say in his heart, My lord delayeth his coming;

49 And shall begin to smite his fellowservants, and to eat and drink with the drunken;

50 The lord of that servant shall come in a day [65]

when he looketh not for him, and in an hour **Mt. 24/50**
that he is not aware of,

And shall cut him asunder, and appoint him **51**
his portion with the hypocrites: there shall be
weeping and gnashing of teeth.

Then shall the kingdom of heaven be lik- **Mt. 25/1**
ened unto ten virgins, which took their
lamps, and went forth to meet the bridegroom.

And five of them were wise, and five were **2**
foolish.

They that were foolish took their lamps, and **3**
took no oil with them:

But the wise took oil in their vessels with their **4**
lamps.

While the bridegroom tarried, they all slum- **5**
bered and slept,

And at midnight there was a cry made, Behold, **6**
the bridegroom cometh; go ye out to meet him.

Then all those virgins arose, and trimmed their **7**
lamps.

And the foolish said unto the wise, Give us of **8**
your oil; for our lamps are gone out.

But the wise answered, saying, Not so; lest **9**
there be not enough for us and you: but go ye
rather to them that sell, and buy for yourselves.

And while they went to buy, the bridegroom **10**
came; and they that were ready went in with
him to the marriage: and the door was shut.

Mt. 25/11 Afterward came also the other virgins, saying, Lord, Lord, open to us.

12 But he answered and said, Verily I say unto you, I know you not.

13 Watch, therefore.

14 For the kingdom of heaven is as a man travelling into a far country, who called his own servants, and delivered unto them his goods.

15 And unto one he gave five talents, to another two, and to another one; to every man according to his several ability; and straightway took his journey. [66]

16 Then he that had received the five talents went and traded with the same, and made them other five talents.

17 And likewise he that had received two, he also gained other two.

18 But he that had received one went and digged in the earth, and hid his lord's money.

19 After a long time the lord of those servants cometh, and reckoneth with them.

20 And so he that had received five talents came and brought other five talents, saying, Lord, thou deliveredst unto me five talents: behold, I have gained beside them five talents more.

21 His lord said unto him, Well done, thou good and faithful servant: thou hast been faithful over a few things, I will make thee ruler over many things: enter thou into the joy of thy lord.

124

He also that had received two talents came and   Mt. 25/22
said, Lord, thou deliveredst unto me two talents: behold, I have gained two other talents
beside them.

His lord said unto him, Well done, good and   23
faithful servant; thou hast been faithful over a
few things, I will make thee ruler over many
things: enter thou into the joy of thy lord.

Then he which had received the one talent came   24
and said, Lord, I knew thee that thou art
an hard man, reaping where thou hast not
sown, and gathering where thou hast not
strawed:

And I was afraid, and went and hid thy talent   25
in the earth: lo, there thou hast that is thine.

His lord answered and said unto him, Thou   26
wicked and slothful servant, thou knewest that
I reap where I sowed not, and gather where I
have not strawed:

[67] Thou oughtest therefore to have put my money   27
to the exchangers, and then at my coming I
should have received mine own with usury.

Take therefore the talent from him, and give it   28
unto him which hath ten talents.

For unto every one that hath shall be given,   29
and he shall have abundance: but from him
that hath not shall be taken away even that
which he hath.

And cast ye the unprofitable servant into outer   30

125

Mt. 25/30 darkness: there shall be weeping and gnashing of teeth.

L. 21/34 And take heed to yourselves, lest at any time your hearts be overcharged with surfeiting, and drunkenness, and cares of this life, and so that day come upon you unawares.

35 For as a snare shall it come on all them that dwell on the face of the whole earth.

36 Watch ye therefore, and pray always, that ye may be accounted worthy to escape all these things that shall come to pass, and to stand before the Son of Man.

Mt. 25/31 When the Son of Man shall come in his glory, and all the holy angels with him, then shall he sit upon the throne of his glory:

32 And before him shall be gathered all nations: and he shall separate them one from another, as a shepherd divideth his sheep from the goats:

33 And he shall set the sheep on his right hand, but the goats on the left.

34 Then shall the King say unto them on his right hand, Come, ye blessed of my Father, inherit the kingdom prepared for you from the foundation of the world:

35 For I was an hungered, and ye gave me meat: I was thirsty, and ye gave me drink: I was a stranger, and ye took me in:

36 Naked, and ye clothed me: I was sick, and ye visited me: I was in prison, and ye came unto me.

[68] Then shall the righteous answer him, saying, **Mt. 25/37**
      Lord, when saw we thee an hungered, and fed
      thee? or thirsty, and gave thee drink?
      When saw we thee a stranger, and took thee in? **38**
      or naked, and clothed thee?
      Or when saw we thee sick, or in prison, and **39**
      came unto thee?
      And the King shall answer and say unto them, **40**
      Verily I say unto you, Inasmuch as ye have
      done it unto one of the least of these my
      brethren, ye have done it unto me.
      Then shall he say also unto them on the left **41**
      hand, Depart from me, ye cursed, into everlast-
      ing fire, prepared for the devil and his angels:
      For I was an hungered, and ye gave me no meat: **42**
      I was thirsty, and ye gave me no drink:
      I was a stranger, and ye took me not in: naked, **43**
      and ye clothed me not: sick, and in prison, and
      ye visited me not.
      Then shall they also answer him, saying, Lord, **44**
      when saw we thee an hungered, or athirst, or a
      stranger, or naked, or sick, or in prison, and did
      not minister unto thee?
      Then shall he answer them, saying, Verily I say **45**
      unto you, Inasmuch as ye did it not to one of
      the least, ye did it not to me.
      And these shall go away into everlasting pun- **46**
      ishment: but the righteous into life eternal.
      After two days was the feast of the passover, **Mk. 14/1**

127

Mk. 14/1 and of unleavened bread: and the chief priests
and the scribes sought how they might take him
by craft, and put him to death.

2 But they said, Not on the feast day, lest there
be an uproar of the people.

3 And being in Bethany in the house of Simon the
leper, as he sat at meat, there came a woman,
having an alabaster box of ointment of spike- [69]
nard very precious; and she brake the box, and
poured it on his head.

4 And there were some that had indignation
within themselves, and said, Why was this
waste of the ointment made?

5 For it might have been sold for more than three
hundred pence, and have been given to the
poor. And they murmured against her.

6 And Jesus said, Let her alone; why trouble ye
her? she hath wrought a good work on me.

7 For ye have the poor with you always, and
whensoever ye will ye may do them good: but
me ye have not always.

8 She hath done what she could: she is come
aforehand to anoint my body to the burying.

Mt. 26/14 Then one of the twelve, called Judas Iscariot,
went unto the chief priests,

15 And said unto them, What will ye give me, and
I will deliver him unto you? And they cove-
nanted with him for thirty pieces of silver.

And from that time he sought opportunity to betray him. Mt. 26/16

Now the first day of the feast of unleavened bread the disciples came to Jesus, saying unto him, Where wilt thou that we prepare for thee to eat the passover? 17

And he said, Go into the city to such a man, and say unto him, The Master saith, My time is at hand; I will keep the passover at thy house with my disciples. 18

And the disciples did as Jesus had appointed them; and they made ready the passover. 19

Now when the even was come, he sat down with the twelve. 20

And there was also a strife among them, which of them should be accounted the greatest, L. 22/24

And he said unto them, The kings of the Gentiles exercise lordship over them; and they that exercise authority upon them are called benefactors. 25

[70] But ye shall not be so: but he that is greatest among you, let him be as the younger: and he that is chief, as he that doth serve. 26

For whether is greater, he that sitteth at meat, or he that serveth? is not he that sitteth at meat? but I am among you as he that serveth. 27

And supper being ended, J. 13/2

He riseth from supper, and laid aside his gar- 4

J. 13/4 ments; and took a towel, and girded himself.

5 After that he poureth water into a basin, and began to wash the disciples' feet, and to wipe them with the towel wherewith he was girded.

6 Then cometh he to Simon Peter: and Peter saith unto him, Lord, dost thou wash my feet?

7 Jesus answered and said unto him, What I do thou knowest not now; but thou shalt know hereafter.

8 Peter saith unto him, Thou shalt never wash my feet. Jesus answered him, If I wash thee not, thou hast no part with me.

9 Simon Peter saith unto him, Lord, not my feet only, but also my hands and my head.

10 Jesus saith to him, He that is washed needeth not save to wash his feet, but is clean every whit: and ye are clean, but not all.

11 For he knew who should betray him; therefore said he, Ye are not all clean.

12 So after he had washed their feet, and had taken his garments, and was set down again, he said unto them, Know ye what I have done to you?

13 Ye call me Master and Lord: and ye say well; for so I am.

14 If I then, your Lord and Master, have washed your feet; ye also ought to wash one another's feet.

15 For I have given you an example, that ye should do as I have done to you.

Verily, verily, I say unto you, The servant is **J. 13/16**
not greater than his lord; neither he that is sent,
greater than he that sent him.

If ye know these things, happy are ye if ye do **17**
them.

[71] When Jesus had thus said, he was troubled in **21**
spirit, and testified, and said, Verily, verily, I
say unto you, that one of you shall betray me.

Then the disciples looked one on another, **22**
doubting of whom he spake.

Now there was leaning on Jesus' bosom one of **23**
his disciples, whom Jesus loved.

Simon Peter therefore beckoned to him, that he **24**
should ask who it should be of whom he spake.

He then lying on Jesus' breast saith unto him, **25**
Lord, who is it?

Jesus answered, He it is, to whom I shall give a **26**
sop, when I have dipped it. And when he had
dipped the sop, he gave it to Judas Iscariot, the
son of Simon.

Therefore, when he was gone out, Jesus said: **31**
A new commandment I give unto you, That ye **34**
love one another; as I have loved you, that ye
also love one another.

By this shall all men know that ye are my dis- **35**
ciples, if ye have love one to another.

Then saith Jesus unto them, All ye shall be of- **Mt. 26/31**
fended because of me this night:

Peter answered and said unto him, Though all **33**

Mt. 26/33 men shall be offended because of thee, yet will I never be offended.

L. 22/33 I am ready to go with thee, both into prison, and to death.

34 And he said, I tell thee, Peter, the cock shall not crow this day before that thou shalt thrice deny that thou knowest me.

Mt. 26/35 Peter said unto him, Though I should die with thee, yet will I not deny thee. Likewise also said all the disciples.

36 Then cometh Jesus with them unto a place called Gethsemane, and saith unto the disciples, Sit ye here, while I go and pray yonder.

37 And he took with him Peter and the two sons [72] of Zebedee, and began to be sorrowful and very heavy.

38 Then saith he unto them, My soul is exceeding sorrowful, even unto death: tarry ye here, and watch with me.

39 And he went a little farther, and fell on his face, and prayed, saying, O my Father, if it be possible, let this cup pass from me: nevertheless not as I will, but as thou wilt.

40 And he cometh unto the disciples, and findeth them asleep, and saith unto Peter, What! could ye not watch with me one hour?

41 Watch and pray, that ye enter not into temptation: the spirit indeed is willing, but the flesh is weak.

He went away again the second time, and **Mt. 26/42** prayed, saying, O my Father, if this cup may not pass away from me, except I drink it, thy will be done.

And he came and found them asleep again: for **43** their eyes were heavy.

And he left them, and went away again, and **44** prayed the third time, saying the same words.

Then cometh he to his disciples, and saith unto **45** them, Sleep on now, and take your rest.

Then Jesus had spoken these words, he **J. 18/1** went forth with his disciples over the brook Cedron, where was a garden, into the which he entered, and his disciples.

And Judas also, which betrayed him, knew the **2** place: for Jesus ofttimes resorted thither with his disciples.

Judas then, having received a band of men and **3** officers from the chief priests and Pharisees, cometh thither with lanterns, and torches and weapons.

[73] Now that he betrayed him gave them a sign, **Mt. 26/48** saying, Whomsoever I shall kiss, that same is he: hold him fast.

And forthwith he came to Jesus, and said, Hail, **49** Master, and kissed him.

And Jesus said unto him, Friend, wherefore art **50** thou come?

Jesus therefore, knowing all things that should **J. 18/4**

133

J. 18/4 come upon him, went forth, and said unto them, Whom seek ye?

5 They answered him, Jesus of Nazareth. Jesus saith unto them, I am he. (And Judas also, which betrayed him, stood with them.)

6 As soon then as he had said unto them, I am he, they went backward, and fell to the ground.

7 Then asked he them again, Whom seek ye? And they said, Jesus of Nazareth.

8 Jesus answered, I have told you that I am he: if, therefore, ye seek me, let these go their way:

Mt. 26/50 Then came they, and laid hands on Jesus and took him.

51 And, behold, one of them which were with Jesus stretched out his hand, and drew his sword, and struck a servant of the high priest, and smote off his ear.

52 Then said Jesus unto him, Put up again thy sword into his place: for all they that take the sword shall perish with the sword.

55 In that same hour said Jesus to the multitudes, Are ye come out as against a thief with swords and staves for to take me? I sat daily with you teaching in the temple, and ye laid no hold on me.

56 Then all the disciples forsook him, and fled.

Mk. 14/51 And there followed him a certain young man, having a linen cloth cast about his naked body: and the young men laid hold on him:

And he left the linen cloth, and fled from them naked. Mk. 14/52

[74] And they that had laid hold on Jesus led him away to Caiaphas the high priest, where the scribes and the elders were assembled. Mt. 26/57

And Simon Peter followed Jesus, and so did another disciple: that disciple was known unto the high priest, and went in with Jesus into the palace of the high priest. J. 18/15

But Peter stood at the door without. Then went out that other disciple, which was known unto the high priest, and spake unto her that kept the door, and brought in Peter. 16

And the servants and officers stood there, who had made a fire of coals; for it was cold: and they warmed themselves: and Peter stood with them, and warmed himself. 18

Then saith the damsel that kept the door unto Peter, Art not thou also one of this man's disciples? He saith, I am not. 17

And Simon Peter stood and warmed himself: they said, therefore, unto him, Art not thou also one of his disciples? He denied it, and said, I am not. 25

One of the servants of the high priest, (being his kinsman whose ear Peter cut off,) saith, Did not I see thee in the garden with him? 26

Peter then denied again: and immediately the cock crew. 27

135

Mt. 26/75 And Peter remembered the words of Jesus, which said unto him, Before the cock crow, thou shalt deny me thrice. And he went out, and wept bitterly.

J. 18/19 The high priest then asked Jesus of his disciples, and of his doctrine.

20 Jesus answered him, I spake openly to the world; I ever taught in the synagogue, and in the temple, whither the Jews always resort; and in secret have I said nothing.

21 Why askest thou me? ask them which heard [75] me, what I have said unto them: behold, they know what I said.

22 And when he had thus spoken, one of the officers which stood by struck Jesus with the palm of his hand, saying, Answerest thou the high priest so?

23 Jesus answered him, If I have spoken evil, bear witness of the evil: but if well, why smitest thou me?

Mk. 14/53 And they led Jesus away to the high priest: and with him were assembled all the chief priests and the elders and the scribes.*

55 And the chief priests and all the council sought for witness against Jesus to put him to death; and found none:

---

*Mr. Jefferson included this verse in the English text but omitted it from the Greek, Latin and French texts, and from the Table of Contents.

For many bare false witness against him, but **Mk. 14/56**
their witness agreed not together.

And there arose certain, and bare false witness **57**
against him, saying,

We heard him say, I will destroy this temple **58**
that is made with hands, and within three days
I will build another made without hands.

But neither so did their witness agree together. **59**

And the high priest stood up in the midst, and **60**
asked Jesus, saying, Answerest thou nothing? **61**
what is it which these witness against thee?

But he held his peace, and answered nothing.
Again the high priest asked him, and said unto
him, Art thou the Christ, the Son of the Blessed?

And he said unto them, If I tell you, ye will not **L. 22/67**
believe:

And if I also ask you, ye will not answer me, nor **68**
let me go.

Then said they all, Art thou then the Son of **70**
God? And he said unto them, Ye say that I am.

Then the high priest rent his clothes, and saith, **Mk. 14/63**
What need we any further witnesses?

Ye have heard the blasphemy: what think ye? **64**
[76] And they all condemned him to be guilty of
death.

And some began to spit on him, and to cover **65**
his face, and to buffet him, and to say unto him,
Prophesy: and the servants did strike him with
the palms of their hands.

137

J. 18/28 Then they led Jesus from Caiaphas unto the hall of judgment, and it was early; and they themselves went not into the judgment hall, lest they should be defiled; but that they might eat the passover.

29 Pilate then went out unto them, and said, What accusation bring ye against this man?

30 They answered and said unto him, If he were not a malefactor, we would not have delivered him up unto thee.

31 Then said Pilate unto them, Take ye him, and judge him according to your law. The Jews therefore said unto him, It is not lawful for us to put any man to death:

33 Then Pilate entered into the judgment hall again, and called Jesus, and said unto him, Art thou the King of the Jews?

34 Jesus answered him, Sayest thou this thing of thyself, or did others tell it thee of me?

35 Pilate answered, Am I a Jew? Thine own nation and the chief priests have delivered thee unto me: what hast thou done?

36 Jesus answered, My kingdom is not of this world. If my kingdom were of this world, then would my servants fight, that I should not be delivered to the Jews: but now is my kingdom not from hence.

37 Pilate therefore said unto him, Art thou a king then? Jesus answered, Thou sayest that I am a

138

king. To this end was I born, and for this cause **J. 18/37**
came I into the world, that I should bear witness unto the truth. Everyone that is of the
truth heareth my voice.

Pilate saith unto him, What is truth? And when **38**
he had said this, he went out again unto the
Jews, and saith unto them, I find in him no fault
at all.

[77] And they were more fierce, saying, He stirreth **L. 23/5**
up the people, teaching throughout all Jewry,
beginning from Galilee to this place.

Then said Pilate unto him, Hearest thou not **Mt. 27/13**
how many things they witness against thee?

When Pilate heard of Galilee, he asked whether **L. 23/6**
the man were a Galilaean.

And as soon as he knew that he belonged unto **7**
Herod's jurisdiction, he sent him to Herod, who
himself also was at Jerusalem at that time.

And when Herod saw Jesus, he was exceeding **8**
glad: for he was desirous to see him of a long
season, because he had heard many things of
him; and he hoped to have seen some miracle
done by him.

Then he questioned with him in many words; **9**
but he answered him nothing.

And the chief priests and scribes stood and **10**
vehemently accused him.

And Herod, with his men of war, set him at **11**
nought and mocked him, and arrayed him in a

L. 23/11 gorgeous robe, and sent him again to Pilate.

12 And the same day Pilate and Herod were made friends together: for before they were at enmity between themselves.

13 And Pilate, when he had called together the chief priests and the rulers and the people,

14 Said unto them, Ye have brought this man unto me, as one that perverteth the people:* and, behold, I, having examined him before you, have found no fault in this man touching those things whereof ye accuse him:

15 No, nor yet Herod: for I sent you to him; and, lo, nothing worthy of death is done unto him.

16 I will, therefore, chastise him, and release him.

Mt. 27/15 Now at that feast the governor was wont to [78] release unto the people a prisoner, whom they would.

16 And they had then a notable prisoner, called Barabbas.

17 Therefore when they were gathered together, Pilate said unto them, Whom will ye that I release unto you? Barabbas, or Jesus which is called Christ?

---

*[A footnote in Mr. Jefferson's handwriting so small as to be almost illegible, and with some words doubtful, reads,] under the Roman law de seditiosis in crucem tollendis. "Digest de poenis L. 48, lit. 19.6. 28.3." capita plectandi cum saepius seditiosa et turbulentia se gesserint, et aliquotione adprehensi clementius in eadem tementate propositi persevenaverint?

For he knew that for envy they had delivered him.

When he was set down on the judgment seat, his wife sent unto him, saying, Have thou nothing to do with that just man: for I have suffered many things this day in a dream because of him.

19

But the chief priests and elders persuaded the multitude that they should ask Barabbas, and destroy Jesus.

20

The governor answered and said unto them, Whether of the twain will ye that I release unto you? They said, Barabbas.

21

Pilate saith unto them, What shall I do then with Jesus which is called Christ? They all say unto him, Let him be crucified.

22

And the governor said, Why, what evil hath he done? But they cried out the more, saying, Let him be crucified.

23

Then released he Barabbas unto them: and when he had scourged Jesus, he delivered him to be crucified.

26

Then the soldiers of the governor took Jesus into the common hall, and gathered unto him the whole band of soldiers.

27

And when they had platted a crown of thorns, they put it upon his head, and a reed in his right hand: and they bowed the knee before him, and mocked him, saying, Hail, King of the Jews!

29

141

Mt. 27/30 And they spit upon him, and took the reed, and smote him on the head.

31 And after that they had mocked him, they took the robe off from him, and put his own raiment on him, and led him away to crucify him.

3 Then Judas, which had betrayed him, when he saw that he was condemned, repented himself, and brought again the thirty pieces of silver to the chief priests and elders, [79]

4 Saying, I have sinned in that I have betrayed the innocent blood. And they said, What is that to us? see thou to that.

5 And he cast down the pieces of silver in the temple and departed, and went and hanged himself.

6 And the chief priests took the silver pieces, and said, It is not lawful for to put them into the treasury, because it is the price of blood.

7 And they took counsel, and bought with them the potter's field, to bury strangers in.

8 Wherefore that field was called, The field of blood, unto this day.

L. 23/26 And as they led him away, they laid hold upon one Simon, a Cyrenian, coming out of the country, and on him they laid the cross, that he might bear it after Jesus.

27 And there followed him a great company of people, and of women, which also bewailed and lamented him.

28 But Jesus turning unto them said, Daughters of

Jerusalem, weep not for me, but weep for your- L. 23/28
selves, and for your children.

For, behold, the days are coming, in the which 29
they shall say, Blessed are the barren, and the
wombs that never bare, and the paps which
never gave suck.

Then shall they begin to say to the mountains, 30
Fall on us; and to the hills, Cover us.

For if they do these things in a green tree, what 31
shall be done in the dry?

And there were also two others, malefactors, 32
led with him to be put to death.

[80] And he bearing his cross went forth into a place J. 19/17
called the place of a skull, which is called in
the Hebrew, Golgotha:

Where they crucified him, and two other with 18
him, on either side one, and Jesus in the midst.

And Pilate wrote a title, and put it on the cross. 19
And the writing was, JESUS OF NAZARETH,
THE KING OF THE JEWS.

This title then read many of the Jews: for the 20
place where Jesus was crucified was nigh to the
city: and it was written in Hebrew, and Greek,
and Latin.

Then said the chief priests of the Jews to Pilate, 21
Write not, The King of the Jews; but that he
said, I am King of the Jews.

Pilate answered, What I have written I have 22
written.

143

J. 19/23 Then the soldiers, when they had crucified Jesus, took his garments, and made four parts, to every soldier a part; and also his coat: now the coat was without seam, woven from the top throughout.

24 They said therefore among themselves, Let us not rend it, but cast lots for it, whose it shall be:

Mt. 27/39 And they that passed by reviled him, wagging their heads,

40 And saying, Thou that destroyest the temple and buildest it in three days, save thyself. If thou be the Son of God, come down from the cross.

41 Likewise also the chief priests mocking him, with the scribes and elders said,

42 He saved others; himself he cannot save. If he be the King of Israel, let him now come down from the cross, and we will believe him.

43 He trusted in God; let him deliver him now, if he will have him: for he said, I am the Son of God.

L. 23/39 And one of the malefactors which were hanged [81] railed on him, saying, If thou be Christ, save thyself and us.

40 But the other answering rebuked him, saying, Dost not thou fear God, seeing thou art in the same condemnation?

41 And we indeed justly; for we receive the due

reward of our deeds: but this man hath done nothing amiss. L. 23/41

Then said Jesus, Father, forgive them; for they know not what they do. 34

Now there stood by the cross of Jesus his mother, and his mother's sister, Mary the wife of Cleophas, and Mary Magdalene. J. 19/25

When Jesus therefore saw his mother, and the disciple standing by, whom he loved, he saith unto his mother, Woman, behold thy Son! 26

Then saith he to the disciple, Behold thy mother! And from that hour that disciple took her unto his own home. 27

And about the ninth hour Jesus cried with a loud voice, saying, Eli, Eli, lama sabachthani? that is to say, My God, My God, why hast thou forsaken me? Mt. 27/46

Some of them that stood there, when they heard that, said, This man calleth for Elias. 47

And straightway one of them ran, and took a spunge, and filled it with vinegar and put it on a reed, and gave him to drink. 48

The rest said, Let be, let us see whether Elias will come to save him. 49

Jesus, when he had cried again with a loud voice, yielded up the ghost. 50

And many women were there beholding afar off, which followed Jesus from Galilee, ministering unto him. 55

Mt. 27/56   Among which was Mary Magdalene, and Mary
the mother of James and Joses, and the mother
of Zebedee's children.

J. 19/31   The Jews, therefore, because it was the prepara-   [82]
tion, that the bodies should not remain upon
the cross on the sabbath day, (for that sabbath
day was an high day,) besought Pilate that their
legs might be broken, and that they might be
taken away.

32   Then came the soldiers, and brake the legs of
and first, and of the other which was crucified
with him.

33   But when they came to Jesus, and saw that he
was dead already, they brake not his legs:

34   But one of the soldiers with a spear pierced his
side, and forthwith came thereout blood and
water.

38   And after this Joseph of Arimathaea, (being a
disciple of Jesus, but secretly for fear of the
Jews,) besought Pilate that he might take away
the body of Jesus: and Pilate gave him leave.
He came therefore, and took the body of Jesus.

39   And there came also Nicodemus, (which at the
first came to Jesus by night,) and brought a
mixture of myrrh and aloes, about an hundred
pound weight.

40   Then took they the body of Jesus, and wound
it in linen clothes with the spices, as the manner of the Jews is to bury.

Now, in the place where he was crucified, there **J. 19/41**
was a garden; and in the garden a new sepulchre,
wherein was never man yet laid.
There laid they Jesus, **42**
And rolled a great stone to the door of the **Mt. 27/60**
sepulchre, and departed.

Jefferson

AND HIS CONTEMPORARIES

JAROSLAV PELIKAN

There has certainly never been a shortage of boldness in the history of biblical scholarship during the past two centuries, but for sheer audacity Thomas Jefferson's two redactions of the Gospels stand out even in that company. It is still a bit overwhelming to contemplate the sangfroid exhibited by the third president of the United States as, razor in hand, he sat editing the Gospels during February 1804, on (as he himself says) "2. or 3. nights only at Washington, after getting thro' the evening task of reading the letters and papers of the day." He was apparently quite sure that he could tell what was genuine and what was not in the transmitted text of the New Testament, and the eventual outcome of his research and reflection is presented here in this volume. As Dickinson Adams put it after studying Jefferson's procedures, "although many distinguished biblical scholars have been daunted by the challenge of disentangling the many layers of the New Testament, the rationalistic Jefferson was supremely confident of his ability to differentiate between the true and the false precepts of Jesus."

In Jefferson's two excursions into New Testament study, *The Philosophy of Jesus of Nazareth* and then, almost two decades later, this version of *The Life and Morals of Jesus of Nazareth Extracted textually from the Gospels in Greek, Latin, French & English*, historical and literary judgments interact with religious and theological ones. The form in which our Gospels were composed by their anonymous authors (the names Matthew, Mark, Luke, and John appearing only in superscriptions which were presumably added later) makes the task of reconciling their narratives both unavoidable and difficult. Already in the second century, Tatian had prepared a combination of the four accounts, usually called *Diatessaron* ("[one] out of four"), which would enjoy quasi-canonical standing in the Syriac church for centuries; and around the year 400 Augustine prepared *De consensu evangelistarum*, often called his "most laborious work," to prove that the Gospel histories did not contradict one another.

Yet unless one is prepared, as Andreas Osiander apparently was in his *Four Books of the Harmony of the Gospels* (Basel, 1537), to regard even the slightest difference between these four accounts as evidence of separate incidents, one is compelled to assume that not all four Gospels, or perhaps even not a single one of the Gospels, can be strictly chronological in their narration. How long did the public ministry of Jesus last, the year or so suggested by the first three Gospels or the three years or so indicated by the sequence of Jewish festivals in the Fourth Gospel? Did he drive the money changers out of the Temple of Jerusalem at the beginning of his career as a teacher (John 2:13–17) or in its final week (Matt. 21:12–13; Mark 11:15–17; Luke 19:45–46), or did he perhaps do it twice? Is the Sermon on the Mount (Matt. 5–7) identical with the Sermon on the Plain (Luke 6:20–49)? And just how many "words on the Cross" were there, the seven that have been hallowed by various musical settings and homiletical-devotional expositions or the less determinate number that comes from a comparison of the Gospel stories, including the intriguing textual variants?

Regardless of dogmatic presuppositions, or for that matter of antidogmatic presuppositions, therefore, every serious reader of the New Testament is confronted with a host of problems in trying to make historical sense of "the life and morals of Jesus of Nazareth." How such a reader copes with those problems will depend on the interaction of various factors,

151

some of them historiographical and some of them theological (and most of them both historiographical and theological). That neither theological orthodoxy nor a reverence for the inspired text has precluded "tampering" can be seen in the variants of the story of the boy Jesus in the Temple, which appears in the second chapter of the Gospel according to Luke. The Greek text quite unambiguously has Mary say to Jesus: "Behold, your father and I have been looking for you anxiously." But that did not prevent a few pious scribes from deciding, in the light of the story of the Annunciation contained in the preceding chapter, that "your father and I" should be replaced by "we," to avoid any impression that Joseph was in fact the natural father of Jesus.

Even a literalistic adherence to "the original text," moreover, does not dispose of the problems, though it does manage to raise a host of new ones. Thus the *pericope adulteriae*, the story of the woman caught in the act of adultery and dragged before Jesus for his judgment, is evidently not an authentic part of that "original text." Printing the story at the beginning of the eighth chapter of the Gospel of John, the Revised Standard Version explains in a footnote: "The most ancient authorities omit 7.53–8.11; other authorities add the passage here or after

7.36 or after 21.25 or after Luke 21.38, with variations of text." Nevertheless, many scholars are convinced that the incident validates itself *prima facie* as an authentic element of the earliest tradition about Jesus, and that it was not, despite the textual problems, a later addition by a church in which, increasingly, many followers of Jesus were showing that they would have been quite willing to "cast the first stone."

Although he did have a keen interest in all sorts of antiquarian questions, Jefferson was not engaging in a "quest for the historical Jesus" primarily as an exercise in historical investigation, any more than were most of the others who participated in that quest during the nineteenth and twentieth centuries. He wanted to find the essence of true religion in the Gospels, an essence whose basic content he had already formulated for himself with considerable simplicity and clarity. Like other Enlightenment rationalists, Jefferson was convinced that the real villain in the Christian story was the apostle Paul, who had corrupted the religion *of* Jesus into a religion *about* Jesus, which thus had, in combination with the otherworldly outlook of the Fourth Gospel, produced the monstrosities of dogma, superstition, and priestcraft, which were the essence of Christian orthodoxy. The essence of authentic religion, and therefore of the only kind of Christianity in which Jefferson was interested, needed to be rescued from these distortions, so that the true person and teaching of Jesus of Nazareth might rise from the dead page—the only kind of resurrection Jefferson was prepared to accept.

It has become customary in our time to speak rather condescendingly about this search for an "essence" within and behind the received forms of the Christian message, with such pejorative terms as "reductionism" springing easily to mind. Yet it bears pointing out that the search is in fact an ancient one, and that it comes with some very impressive credentials. "He has showed you, O man, what is good; and what does the Lord require of you but to do justice, and to love kindness, and to walk humbly with your God?" the prophet Micah declared. The writer of the Epistle to the Hebrews likewise asserted that "whoever would draw near to God must believe that he exists and that he rewards those who seek him." And when Jesus was approached with the stock rabbinical question about which was the great commandment in the law, he did not, according to the Gospels, reject the question as reductionist, but stood it on its head by making love to God and love to neighbor coordinate. This is not to say that Jefferson's version of the "essence" is automatically legitimate, but the impulse to look for an irreducible minimum in the welter of belief and practice cannot be waved aside as reductionism.

The Enlightenment of the eighteenth century, of which Thomas Jefferson was in his own highly individual fashion both a pupil and an exponent, brought to this assignment a new interest in history as an instrument for clarification and liberation. In the well-known contrast drawn by his contemporary, Edward Gibbon, "the theologian may indulge the pleasing task of describing Religion as she descended from Heaven, arrayed in her native purity. A more melancholy duty is imposed on the historian. He must discover the inevitable mixture of error and corruption which she contracted in a long residence upon earth, among a weak and degenerate race of beings"; Gibbon left no doubt about where his own sympathies lay between the two, and they were sympathies that Jefferson shared. And when, moreover, Gibbon described history as "indeed, little more than the register of the crimes, follies, and misfortunes of mankind," that, too, at least as it pertained to most ancient monarchies and institutional churches, was a sentiment in which Jefferson would have concurred. It was the historian's task to penetrate the layers of myth and propaganda and to find the real truth of history.

Applied to the history of Christianity, that task entailed the abolition of the privileged sanctuary in which the writers and events of the Bible had been reposing for centuries, as well as the application to them of the same critical methodologies that pertained to any honest historiography. Significantly, that principle was easier and "safer" to carry out in studying the Old Testament than the New, and within the New Testament in interpreting the Epistles than in analyzing the Gospels. Not without touches of anti-Semitic condescension, radical critics set the "tribal religion of Jehovah" into opposition with the higher and more universal (that is to say, more rationalistic and less specifically Jewish) religion allegedly espoused by the Minor Prophets. They went on to draw a similar opposition between the universal religion of Jesus and the Christian particularity of the religion of Paul. Combining these two emphases, Jefferson thus made Jesus into "the greatest of all the Reformers of the depraved religion of his own country," but Paul into the "first corrupter of the doctrines of Jesus."

To put this version of *The Life and Morals of Jesus of Nazareth* into historical context, it is instructive to compare the approach of Thomas Jefferson (1734–1826) to the central issues with those of several of his contemporaries, older and younger, who likewise addressed themselves to these issues. In chronological order, they are Hermann Samuel Reimarus (1694–1768), David Hume (1711–76), Johann Wolfgang von Goethe (1749–1832), and John Henry Newman (1801–90).

Of the four, Hermann Samuel Reimarus was the closest to Jefferson in the intellectual and scholarly enterprise of probing for the real man Jesus of Nazareth behind the figure in the Gospels. It is noteworthy that Albert Schweitzer's *The Quest of the Historical Jesus* begins with him; the German title of Schweitzer's book is *Von Reimarus zu Wrede*. Reimarus did not, however, carry out his own reconstruction of "the life and morals of Jesus of Nazareth" by resorting to the draconian measure of expunging from the text what apparently did not belong there, so as, in Jefferson's choice phrase, to separate the "diamonds" from the "dung." Instead, Reimarus labored for many years on an *Apology or Defense of the Rational Worshipers of God* (a title that Jefferson would have found congenial), the fundamental section of which bore the title: "On the Intention of Jesus and of His Disciples." As Reimarus read the story, the teachings of Jesus were an uneasy amalgam of a universal, rational religion with remnants of the religion of Israel. His "intention," accordingly, also combined a message of the pure, nonceremonial worship of the one God with a belief in apocalyptic intervention by the God of Israel and a consequent establishment of the kingdom of God on earth. This kingdom, Jesus believed, would come into being through him. To that belief he clung to the very end, and the cry of dereliction on the cross, "My God, my God, why hast thou forsaken me?" with its echoes of Psalm 22, was his heartbroken scream of despair when he finally had to recognize that the theocracy of which he had dreamed would never come true. Nevertheless, Reimarus insisted, the abiding relevance of the message of Jesus was not dependent on this vain hope, nor was it vitiated by the tragedy of the cross. For at its center, that message corresponded to the best that had been taught by all the saints and sages of human history, and to the deepest intuitions of the human heart; and therefore it was eternal.

The most striking difference between the picture drawn by Reimarus and Jefferson's interpretations, however, was in the mode of their dissemination. For although, as Dumas Malone points out in his magisterial biography,

Jefferson "made no effort to clarify his own position or make his personal religious opinions
known [because] ... he regarded this as a
wholly private matter which was nobody's business but his," he did not on the other hand
attempt to keep the radical Deism of his theological views secret. By contrast, Reimarus remained a closet Deist all his life. He published
a mildly rationalistic defense of more or less
traditional beliefs about "natural religion,"
while at the same time he was secretly writing
his iconoclastic portrait of Jesus the failure.
Only after his death did portions of the work
see the light of day, through the efforts of the
German philosopher and man of letters, Gott-
hold Ephraim Lessing (1729–81), who published them between 1774 and 1778 as anonymous "fragments" from the library at
Wolfenbüttel. There were, of course, obvious
political reasons for this difference between the
publication of the two reconstructions of Gospel tradition. Even in the Protestant Germany
of the *Aufklärung* there would have been great
professional and economic risk if a professor of
Hebrew at the University of Hamburg had gone
public with such extreme views. Jefferson was
running considerably less risk in America, although, as he discovered in his campaigns for
the presidency, it was still politically dangerous

to be a theological heretic. At the same time, it also bears noting that the posthumous publication of the work of Reimarus created a major stir among theologians and scholars, in a way that the "amateurish" work of his younger and more famous contemporary in Monticello did not.

The "natural religion" that so preoccupied both Reimarus and Jefferson was also a theme to which David Hume gave frequent and careful attention. In Jefferson's judgment, to be sure, his contemporary David Hume did not belong to what he called the "trinity of the three greatest men the world has ever produced," namely, Sir Francis Bacon, Sir Isaac Newton, and John Locke (all three of them British, by the way); for it was these three who had "laid the foundation of those superstructures which have been raised in the physical and moral sciences." Hume's *Dialogues Concerning Natural Religion*—which, like the *Apology* of Reimarus, was published posthumously— probed the attempts to use human reason and experience as the foundation for a consistent interpretation of the world and of God as "a necessarily existent being," as the philosophical theologians of the Enlightenment had been articulating it. The presumption of human reason in asserting "the moral attributes of the Deity, his justice, benevolence, mercy, and rectitude, to be of the same nature with these virtues in human creatures" was sheer "anthropomorphism." Much of the polemic in Hume's *Dialogues Concerning Natural Religion* was specifically aimed at "the ignorance of these reverent gentlemen" among the clergy who continued to make such presumptuous claims for the apologetic enterprise as a prop for orthodox Christian doctrine. But by the time Hume had finished his devastating critique of these claims, he had no less thoroughly disposed of Enlightenment rationalism. Indeed, as he added in a footnote, "it seems evident, that the dispute between the sceptics and dogmatists is entirely verbal."

And that would seem to be an attack no less upon Jefferson's kind of rationalism than upon that of his more orthodox opponents. As has already been suggested, Jefferson was proceeding here in *The Life and Morals of Jesus of Nazareth* on a twofold assumption, which he believed to be ultimately a single assumption: that it was possible, on the basis of reason and without recourse to the notion of special revelation, to know those few universal truths about God and the world and the relation between them that were necessary for a responsible moral life; and that the wisest teachers of the human race,

161

among whom Jesus of Nazareth was preeminent if not unique, had known and promulgated these truths, even though their disciples and followers had often intermingled "dung" with these "diamonds." Because Jefferson was so sure of the first of these assumptions, he could be as confident as he was in applying the second to the Gospels. But if Hume was right in questioning the logical validity of a rationally demonstrable "natural religion," the use of it as a touchstone for sorting out the deeds and sayings of the Gospel tradition must also come into question. Among Christian theologians, especially on the European Continent, Immanuel Kant's (1724–1804) continuation and clarification of Hume's insights into the limitations of reason was in many ways more influential; but taken together, their analyses would make increasingly difficult the simplistic hermeneutical procedures to which Jefferson resorted in his version of "the quest of the historical Jesus."

Theologically the most influential of all of Jefferson's contemporaries on the European Continent was, if not Immanuel Kant, then almost certainly Johann Wolfgang von Goethe. Throughout the rest of the nineteenth century, his philosophy of nature and art permeated the systems of writers and thinkers—"Dichter und Denker"—throughout the West. It was

162

Goethe's bust that Ralph Waldo Emerson put on his mantel, Goethe's *Theory of Colours* (translated into English) that J. M. W. Turner annotated about 1840 as he was working out his own doctrines of color and light, Goethe's conclusion to *Faust* that V. S. Soloviev (arguably the greatest of all Russian philosophers) printed as the epigraph for one of his most important books. And Goethe shared with Jefferson the effort to combine a specific reverence for "the life and morals of Jesus of Nazareth" with a universalism about the strivings and achievements of the human spirit that could not confine its loyalty to any single teacher, not even to Jesus.

The universalism came to voice throughout Goethe's vast authorship, but above all in *Faust*, which opens like the Book of Job and closes like Dante's *Paradiso*, using the old legend of the sorcerer Faust to affirm the human quest for salvation and meaning—but a salvation and meaning available to all who would, by their striving, assert and fulfill their essential humanity. Like Jefferson in his recension of the Gospels, Faust found the story of the resurrection of Jesus unbelievable, attractive though it might be, but retained an eschatological hope for an *apokatastasis pantōn* ("restoration of all things") in which everyone could share. *Faust* is the account of a compact with the Devil for the sake of knowledge and pleasure, but its denouement is a triumph over the Devil and a redemption from sin and error, in which the innocent suffering of Gretchen and the power of her intercession save her betrayer from the consequences of his own folly: "Everything transient is only a parable, the Eternal Feminine leads us upward."

Hovering over that closing scene of Goethe's *Faust* is the mystical figure of Mary—"Virgin, Mother, Queen, Goddess!"—but the figure of Jesus is much more difficult to identify. Yet Goethe's preoccupation with the figure of Jesus was, quite literally, lifelong. On 11 March 1832, just eleven days before his death, Goethe declared in his *Conversations with Eckermann*: "Beyond the grandeur and the moral elevation of Christianity, as it sparkles and shines in the Gospels, the human mind will not advance." Traditional Christianity had sought to preserve that sense of grandeur by encasing the Jesus of the Gospels in the christological dogma of the two natures, as confessed by the Council of Chalcedon in 451. But Goethe, like his slightly older contemporary Jefferson, was convinced that this grandeur, "as it sparkles and shines in the Gospels," was self-authenticating and that it did not need the artificial props of creed, dogma, and liturgy.

Quite the opposite view was espoused by Jefferson's and Goethe's far younger contemporary, John Henry Newman, whose life spanned almost the entire nineteenth century. He, too, was endlessly fascinated by "the grandeur and the moral elevation of Christianity, as it sparkles and shines in the Gospels"; but for him, as he acknowledged in his *Apologia pro vita sua*, "from the age of fifteen dogma has been the fundamental principle of my religion: I know no other religion." Newman was well aware of the literary and historical problems in the composition, collection, and interpretation of the books of the Bible. He also knew, not only historically and philosophically but existentially, the meaning and the power of doubt as a pervasive force in the human mind, and he formulated his most profound and subtle book, *An Essay in Aid of a Grammar of Assent*, as an argument for the compatibility of authentic faith with the lack of the kind of absolute intellectual certainty to which, in traditional apologetics, it is often tied. What brought them together was the reality and power of the Church and of its developing tradition, as that tradition had expressed itself in the Gospels and as it would go on expressing itself in the very creed, dogma, and liturgy that Jefferson found so distasteful.

In that same work, Newman also took up, in an argument with the famous discussion about the causes of the success of Christianity in Edward Gibbon's *The Decline and Fall of the Roman Empire*, what he himself believed to be the central explanation of that success: the Image of Christ, as a principle of association which brings his followers together into the Church as the Body of Christ, and also as the foundation of their moral life. "It was," Newman concluded against Gibbon, "the Thought of Christ, not a corporate body or a doctrine, which inspired that zeal which the historian so poorly comprehends; and it was the Thought of Christ which gave a life to the promise of that eternity, which without Him would be, in any soul, nothing short of an intolerable burden." From that perspective, of course, the wedge that Jefferson sought to drive between the historical Jesus and his followers in succeeding generations was unthinkable: the only Jesus to whom we have access is the Christ of the Church, the Gospels were compiled in the light of the faith of the Church, and the dogma and liturgy of the Church are the key to the faithful interpretation of "the life and morals of Jesus of Nazareth." Even the gainsayers of dogma would not have the Gospels they use as weapons against it if those Gospels had not been faithfully preserved by the Church.

These similarities and differences between Jefferson and his contemporaries are a testimony to the hold that the figure of the Man in the Gospels continues to have over human hearts and minds, but they also provide a perspective on the heart and mind of one bold and sensitive man who, in his own special way, also wanted to be this Man's disciple and contemporary.

Index OF EXTRACTS

FROM THE NEW TESTAMENT

I N D E X   O F   E X T R A C T S

être
the cow

être
the cow

sean kenniff

Health Communications, Inc.
Deerfield Beach, Florida

www.hcibooks.com

This is a work of fiction. Any resemblance to actual cows or other farm animals, living or dead, is purely coincidental.

Library of Congress Cataloging-in-Publication Data

Kenniff, Sean.
    Être the cow / Sean Kenniff.
        p. cm.
    ISBN-13: 978-0-7573-1502-2
    ISBN-10: 0-7573-1502-X
    1. Cows—Fiction.   2. Experimental fiction.   I. Title.
PS3611.E668E87 2010
813'.6—dc22

                                                            2009046975

Publisher: Health Communications, Inc.
              3201 S.W. 15th Street
              Deerfield Beach, FL 33442–8190

Edited by Carol A. Rosenberg
Cover design by Larissa Hise Henoch
Interior design and formatting by Dawn Von Strolley Grove

This is a story about a cow.

Or not.

"Moo!"

This happens so often I rarely take notice. Girls and men, boys and women call out to me, and to every one of us here, from outside this fence of wire and wood confining my pasture.

"Moo, cow!" they shout, and I try not to turn. But I do, and as always, I am humiliated. They call out to my hoofed legs, the flies on my haunches, and the grass in my mouth. They cry at my stinking cowness. I am a bull, not a cow. But I am a beast and so are the others, and the shame of this burns like the sunshine on my back.

It's more crowded than ever on the pasture, and I can't count us all—a few brutes, perhaps a few hundred broads and their calves. All the good grasses been chewed long ago and now we have only yellowed patches to fill our bellies.

I haven't eaten a daffodil in several seasons.

When the rain comes, brilliant green sprouts burst through puddles and dung and dirt but are quickly trampled by the curious and careless. None of us here are patient. The men on the horses with their grinning dogs will soon come and move us all to better land, and we will eat without rest. If they don't move us, we'll starve. And if we starve, they starve, that's my understanding of things. So I wait, with the others. They call this place Gorwell Farm, and I call myself être. It's the only word I can say.

I don't reckon they say. But I do reckon. I'm not sure how long I've been doing that. It's hard for me to tell. It's like a cocoon just splits open one summer, a butterfly beats its wings and zigzags away. To the butterfly, the caterpillar never really figures. That's how it happens, I think.

"Unghf," I say and swallow the blades on my tongue.

"Unghf," a nearby bull answers.

"Anghf," a cow says.

The ants are on the move again, snaking their way through the grass in a jagged line. They pay me no notice even as I loom above them. In one direction most are hauling tiny bits of world in their pincers—leaves, insect wings, rotting pulp of apricot, and globs of mud. I follow one of them. He cuts under the thickets, over sticks, and in and out of cow tracks, holding a mantis head in his jaws. The mantis eyes look at me and I look away. I'm careful where I step when I follow. The ant disappears, and I push blades of grass out of the way with my face so he does not get lost to me. Along the path, ants crawling in the other direction meet this one, touch him, flail their antennae, and then move on. I nudge two sluggish broads with dim eyes out of the way; they are slow to move. I find my ant again. In the clearing he crawls faster and straighter. And when he finally arrives at his home, he drops out of sight down the hole. I wait. Then I decide to stop waiting, and I plough one of my hooves through his mound. This gets all the ants excited. They storm up my legs, bite at my flesh, and taste my enormity. To them I am incomprehensible, and after a while they leave me be.

"Unghf," I say, and pull roots from the dirt.

Many in the herd are moving to the water at the long end of the pasture, where side by side they'll gulp from the stream until they are fat and slow. On hotter days some will even stand in it. Water looks more interesting when a cow is standing in it. And I like to look at that. But this day it's not that hot.

I don't much like going to the stream ever since my first time. I was smaller then, and I recall I got there just like the others—I followed. I slipped and crouched and bent my way between hundreds of cows, and then stretched my neck long until I reached the water's edge. But my legs buckled. Under the water the most awful beast eyed me like it had been waiting for me all along: this hideous water-cow.

"Mneweh," I turned to the others, using a cry only calves can cry.

For certain, the others had seen the water-cow. But they stood calm. So I crept back to the water's edge and peaked in again. I didn't go so far as to see its horrible face, but when I saw those ragged ears flickering on the surface, I thrashed my body backward. I turned, pushing and twisting my way between so many cows, and I ran from the stream until my legs folded.

Later, when the other cows lumbered back to the pasture one by one, I walked back to the stream alone and again the water-cow was waiting for me.

He had a rotten-apple nose, black and wet. Ears like mangled leaves. Two bird-egg eyeballs low on his head jutting from the sides of the skull. His hide was clay colored, not the rusty brown, black, or white I'd seen on the other cows, just the color of water-meets-earth. Like me the water-cow was a bull, or turning into one, with stubs for horns. His tongue, brown and thick and mottled, hung limply out of the side of his mouth. I moved my head this way, then that way, then this way again, and so did the water-cow. I snorted and so did the water-cow. His ears flicked. So did mine. I dipped my face into the water; he poked his face out. Our noses touched.

"Unghf," I bellowed, and so did he.

I was this water-cow, he was me, and we were gruesome.

As a calf, I would hide my face against my mother's milky belly. But without her there is no hiding me. I'm a horrible cow, it's true, the ugliest bull on the pasture, and I prefer to do my drinking at puddles of fallen rainwater.

They bring the sun up, heating the other cows from their sleep. All night I walked among the heaving bodies until my thoughts lost shape in the light, having gone where the moon goes. I rest against a fence post and rub my hide until it stings.

A door closes at the barn with a creak and clank. Farmer Creely is walking his boy and his dog. The boy is kind and I don't much mind Farmer Creely. But that dog, I hate. Never met a dog I liked. Most of them not even as high as my belly but they chase us into big groups, snarling and nipping at us even as we run. Cows and bulls can't outrun dogs. They're there, then here, then there, then wherever we turn, and some days they taunt us without mercy. There are no bulls on the pasture when those dogs are around; we're all cows then.

The farmer and his dog walk down the trail on the side

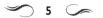

of the road, leaving the boy by a post at the fence. I walk near.

"Jacques," the farmer says, "you comin' with?"

"No, can I stay here 'n look at the cows?"

"Suit yerself. But lookin' don't make a farmer now. Does it?"

"No, Paw."

"Doin' does, Jacques. Doin' makes a farmer."

"I know, Paw," the boy says.

"We got to feed the pigs first, Jacques," the farmer says. "Pigs come first."

"Uh huh."

"Now you stay right there while I tend the hog feed."

"'K, Paw."

"Don't go off now, y'hear?"

"I won't, Paw."

"Right then."

"Right, Paw."

The farmer lifts a stick from the side of the trail and throws it high and far. The dog runs after it like it's got no mind.

I go close. "être," I say to the boy.

"Shoo, cow," he says, rattling the fence, "yah, shoo!" and tosses a few stones against me. He must be thinking I'm one of the other cows, but I shoo away a little on account of the stones and turn my face to the pasture to chew.

The farmer's boy doesn't much come inside the pasture. If he did, I'd try to get up good and close with him. He's mighty small, compared to Farmer Creely and us cows anyhow. So most times the boy just sets himself up near the fence and plays with dirt and sticks and bugs, like I like to do. When the men and the dogs aren't around, the boy sings. Sometimes the farmer and the other men catch him singing, and they listen along without him knowing. But other times they tell him to stop his singing and stop bothering us cows. He's no bother to me or the others from what I can tell, but he won't sing for days after that. The boy's got a lot of songs inside. I have songs inside me too, but I reckon I'll never get a single one of them out speaking as I do.

I hear the boy's song, and I turn. His hair, yellowed as our grass, shades his face from the sun.

> *Alouette, gentille Alouette*
> *Alouette—je te plumerai*
> *Alouette, gentille Alouette*
> *Alouette—je te plumerai*
> *Je te plumerai la tête*
> *Je te plumerai la tête*
> *Et la tête, et la tête*

Alouette, Alouette
O-o-o-o-oh-Alouette, gentille Alouette
Alouette—je te plumerai

He stops singing. He looks at me with his raindrop eyes and my face heats.

"Keep singing."

But he goes silent. I chew and snap my tail. He sings again, but more quiet now, and I have to stop breathing just to hear him.

Je te plumerai le nez
Je te plumerai le nez
Et le nez, et le nez
O-o-o-o-oh-Alouette, gentille
Alouette.*

That's the kind of song I'd like to sing I think, and I move my mouth up and back and show my teeth. I dip my head and roll my tongue this way, then that way, then this way again, and show my teeth once more. Other cows are moving past, lots of them, and they see me doing this. This is another horrible day. But the song is with me now; I can hear it just fine inside my cowhead, and walking away from the boy, I sing it best I can.

* For English translation see page 129.

chaptêr two

N ew cows with craggy brown faces stagger off two big trucks all mussed up, like the dogs have been chasing them in the dark. The chute runs off the trucks are violent and short with cows balking and bucking the whole way down. They make so much racket it blinds me for a while. Some of the new cows collapse as soon as they touch the ground and just lay there, cow folded into cow. But other new cows run angry, especially the bulls, kicking and charging and that makes all us cows angry.

"Unnnnnghf, unnnnnnnghf, unnnnnnnnghff!"

Then it starts like always—bulls charge bulls. Cows charge bulls. Bulls charge cows, and all of us charge calves. With so many cows running around in roaring clouds of hides and horns, I lose my eyes, I lose my ears, and my tongue grows dry and heavy with dust.

WhoaCowsWhoaCowsWhoaCowsWhoaCowsWhoa-Cows! I hear from someplace else. Hoof after hoof mash what little good grasses we got into the dirt, or rip them up from the roots in big patches—and no cow, old or new, got any sense about it. Not even me. I run and charge as a cow too; this way, then that way, then this way again, and all over this pasture. I run from fear and I run to fear. The men and dogs shout from the fence, but it doesn't stop us. For half the day the ground quakes in grotesque shame until all us cows settle.

After it all I can hardly move in the center of the cow pack. I strain to lift my head as high as I can. I'm stuck here. We're all too close, and I stare into the rump of a brown bull whose tail is snapping from side to side. He's anxious. Flies dart from his dirty haunches to my face, into my eyes, and into my mouth. Bulls should never be this close. I think. I lower my head. I am thirsty but the grass is dry.

I close my eyes and let all the air out of my chest.

"Unghf."

There's a lot of comings and goings at Gorwell. A few steer have been here as long as I have but none of them cows stay around for long. The calves come and go about as often. The men just ride their horses in here like thunder on rainstorms, with their dogs rounding us up—calves, cows, and bulls alike. There's no telling when they're coming, just a day like any other. You're chewing grass or just thinking about it, then they got you on the run in all sorts of ways, scrambling about. That's how it goes. Some of us are dog-chased to the better grasses;

others are kept here on grasses already eaten.

On occasion, some cows, calves, and a bull or two are chased into the corral where they feed for many days from the farmer's trough. I don't know what kind of feed the farmer puts in that trough, but the cows grow big and fat in the corral. And all us other cows, even the ones on good grasses, don't like them much for doing that— getting fat like they do in plain view of us all. Sometimes I anger so much I'd charge them over and over if I could. But I suppose outside the fences cows got endless green grasses to chew 'cause they never come back here. After some time when they are fattened to the farmer's liking, the corral cows are herded into that long curved chute by the road, and one by one they walk into that birch-wood building at the far end of the pasture, close to where they bring the sun down.

So many gone in that way, I can't recall a single cow but my mother.

Cows aren't much company anyways, so I don't really mind all those comings and goings. I surely don't know what I'd do without that boy, though. He's been around about as long as me, and longer than most cows on the pasture. He never hears me right, or maybe he just doesn't want to listen to my cowtalk. I reckon he has nothing to learn from a cow with one good word to say. But I hear him right and good, and by listening to him, the farmer, and some of the farmer's men, I mostly learn my words. Only the boy knows songs. Cows don't sing or even talk—least as far as I can tell, but I'm plenty sure they hear 'cause none of us like noise. But I suppose words and songs just don't go deep enough for the other cows.

I pull up close to a milker. She's eating and guarding some remains of yellowed grass. She's almost as big as me but chicken white with a speckled peach nose. She's got swollen udder and one of her teats blown up pink. She stops chewing when I come close, and I stop moving.

"Unghf," I say.

Her tail twitches and she lifts her head, then drops it again. I show her my sides.

"Unghf," I say again, flick my ears and move toward her slow.

"Anghf," she says, then goes quiet.

I take a few more steps, and I nudge her neck with my nose.

"Unghf," I say, and nudge again. She bends to eat grasses. "Unghf," I say. But the cow says nothing. I stand and I wait. I lift one front hoof and hold it up. I show her because this is no problem for me. I bend and eat grasses with just my three hoofs to the ground. I chew.

"Unghf," I say, dropping my hoof.

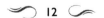

When the milker looks at me, I turn to her head on to look at her square. Flicking my ears I try to get her to talk with me.

"Those men should come soon and move us to the better grass."

Nothing.

"I hunger and thirst."

Nothing.

"I think they'll be coming soon."

Nothing.

"Do you hear?"

And I wait.

The milker's tongue is meaty and coarse, rasping against her snout as she chews cud, grassy juices dribbling from the corners of her mouth.

"Unghf," I say. "You're a stupid ugly cow."

Nothing.

"You dirty the same grasses you eat. You even serve the flies—just like I do."

"Unghf!" I hear, but much louder than my own.

I turn. A large black bull is standing behind me. He breathes heavy at me. He lowers his head and shows me his side. His horns are long and sharp, turning inward. He curves his back up and the little hairs along his spine rise. He lifts his head, updown, updown, updown. "Unghf," he says. "Unghf!"

"Unghf," I say back. I lower my head, draw down my ears, and step back a bit from the milker. I don't mean trouble, and I reckon she is rightly his cow.

"Unghf," he huffs.

"Can you hear me, Black Bull?"

He lowers his head and digs at the soil with his front hoof.

"Do you even know what you are?"

Nothing.

"Your life is a curse."

Nothing.

"You just have no mind about it."

He charges me.

"être!" I say, and I run. "Listen to me! Listen to me, listen to me! Cows hear me!" But with those words locked in my cow body, I cannot stir them, and I shout the only word I got, my name.

"Coohoo, coohoo, coohoo," the chickens say, but there's no sense to any of it.

I poke my head out of the pasture through the fence wires close to the chicken pen, and they scatter, flapping their wings wildly. The top wire rips into my ear as it always does, and I will tear the other ear when I pull myself back inside. I know this much. Such desires pain us cows, but the grass on the strip between the pasture and the pen is green and long and delicious with no other cows chewing on it or otherwise disgracing it. Even the air out on the strip has only a hint of cow, and I breathe it in large gulps. When the pain in my ear subsides, I dig my face into the grass and pull the thick blades out of the soil. The chickens pitch themselves up and down, sending white feathers into the air.

"Coohoo! Coohoo!" they warn.

Can't talk sense to them chickens, it's no use. Only chickens are more lowly than us cows, walking on two legs like men but cursed with wings that will never fly.

"Coohoo, coohoo!" the chickens scream.

"Unghf," I say, and I chew.

"Owf! Owf! Owf!" a filthy dirt-colored dog darts over, snarling and barking at my massive grass-poaching cowhead, and sending the chickens into more flapping foolishness.

"Coohoo! Coohoo!"

"OwfOwfOwfOwfOwfOwfOwfOwfOwf!"

Dogs have sharp teeth, and I've known a few to use them. I try to pull back, but my head is caught.

"Coohoo! Coohoo!"

"Unghf," I say to the dog, but he keeps barking at me, bouncing on his front paws with his hind in the air.

"Whiiirp!" the farmer whistles. "Get along now Rexy and leave the cow be!"

"OwfOwfOwfOwfOwfOwfOwfOwfOwf!"

"Unghf."

"Coohoo! Coohoo!"

"OwfOwfOwfOwfOwf!"

"Rexy!" the farmer shouts.

"Owf! Owf!"

"C'mon, boy! C'meer, Rexy," the boy says.

"Owf! Owf!"

The farmer whistles again, the dog leaves me be, and I chew good grass. The farmer stops so close to me he blocks the sun, and his boy follows. I try to pay them no mind, and I move the cud around my mouth and I swallow.

"A fine mess you're in here, cow."

"I think his head is stuck," the boy says.

"Yeah, I reckon it is," the farmer says. "Well let's let him be. He figured how to get his head through the fence, he'll figure how to get his head back in."

"You think?"

"'Spose he will."

The boy begins to laugh. This is the very best sound the boy makes, and I stop chewing to watch him.

"You seeing something funny here, Jacques?"

"He looks so," the boy snorts, "he looks so, he looks so . . . stupid," and then explodes in laughter.

"Unghf," I say, which makes the boy laugh even harder.

"Shush now, Jacques, shush yerself! You don't want to spook him with a head stuck like that. He'll likely hurt himself or end up pulling the whole side of fence down."

"Sorry, Paw! It's just, it's just, it . . . "

"Shush now. Cows don't know right from wrong, up from down, shit from sunshine. But this one here looks rightly smart. He's trying to get at the good grass here, see? None of them other cows figuring that sorta thing out, now are they?"

"'Spose no."

"'Spose no is right, boy, and besides, cows ain't so dumb as people think. They get along best they know how, just like you and me. They know cowin', we know farmin', bugs know buggin'. And that's how it goes. Come on now, leave him be."

"But what if he's really stuck?"

"And what if he is?"

"Won't he choke and die?"

"Reckon he might, but that don't change much, we got

lots of cows. Besides, he'll die happy eating all that good grass. C'mon, Jacques, he'll be fine, leave him, we got work waitin'," the farmer says, walking away. "Jacques?"

The boy moves closer to my head and reaches slowly for the top wire. I lift my head to feel him and he recoils, knotting his tiny hands together against his chest.

"Jacques? I said the cow'll be fine. Leave him be."

"But, Paw, what if he can't . . . "

"He can, son. He can, and he will."

The boy still won't leave me, so the farmer comes back, moving him aside.

"Okay, cow, back where you belong," the farmer says, lifting the wire over my horns. He cups my wounded ear with his other hand; it is hard like wood, and he pushes my cowhead back where it belongs. I look out at them from inside the pasture.

"Don't he look sadder to you now, son?" the farmer says.

"Reckon he does."

"I reckon he does too. Leave him be, let's go now."

"Coohoo, coohoo, coohoo," the chickens say.

"'K, Paw."

"'K now, let's move on," the farmer says, and with the dog grinning between his legs, they walk off.

Just before the sun's brought down for good, three of the farmer's men open up the gate, secure it once more, and come inside the pasture. With the sun low behind them I can't make out their faces, hard as I try, just three flame-colored shadows, one with a rifle slung up over his shoulder. The men talk close to each other as they move through the herd and stop behind one of the new cows. She's sprawled out sickly on the dirt and been that way all day long, ever since the truck brought her here. The farmer and his men don't much like it when cows don't stand or eat on their own, this much I know.

"Stand up." But she doesn't get up.

Two men stoop by her haunches while the gun man stands behind her head. They all keep far from her legs, with good reason. When the cow turns her head and sees those men standing so close, she flails her legs like a foal learning to walk and tries to right herself. She grunts unlike a cow and pushes hard against the earth but can't hold herself steady. Her front legs split, smashing her throat and mouth into the ground. Her back legs tremble with the force of it all.

"Anghf," the cow cries.

"Looks like Chapel Farms sold us another downer," says one of the farmer's men.

"Seems so."

"Yup."

The cow struggles to stand, leaning and then circling to one side. The men push with their backs against her ribs to stop her from tipping over, but she crashes to the ground anyway and fully rolls over in a cloud of dust. The men try to hoist her haunches from her other side, but the cow pushes back against them, knifing at the dirt with her hooves.

"Let's give her one more go," says the gun man, and the other two scoop their arms under her backside and try to lift her, but their feet slide in the mud against her weight. The cow breathes deep.

"Alright, I guess that does it."

"Yeah, she's not getting up."

"I'll call the lift?"

"Do that, it's getting dark, and we should get her to processing before they shut down."

"Yeah, damn shame though."

"Shame it is," the gun man says and aims the rifle at the back of the cow's head. The cow draws her legs under herself, turns on her belly, and pushes up with one last shudder.

When the gun fires, the herd startles, the cow's legs stiffen then go limp, and in the flash of the rifle, I can see the men clearly.

chaptêr three

At the top of the small hill in the center of the pastures, I rest myself under a dead oak tree, and its leafless branches curl over my head like terrific horns. With no grass, no water, and little shade, few cows ever come to this place. Here, I can spend my days alone with my hunger and my thirst, and trace all the pasture fences to the green grasses growing beyond them. Only from here can I see the barn, the road, the chicken pen, the stream, and the birch-wood building. Only from here can I see the horses eating pale yellow hay in the stable while the dogs pounce through the buckwheat fields. Only from here can I see Farmer Creely on the porch of the wooden house learning his boy. Only from here can I look down on all the other cows with ease.

Black Bull is in a fury.

"Unghf!" he lowers his horns and shows his broadside.

Being a new bull in this crowded pasture has Black Bull out of sorts. His cows stay close, but some of the other bulls are looking for good cows too. White Face Bull, Small Black Bull, Big Hump Bull, and Broken Eye Bull are challenging Black Bull's claim to his broads. The bulls show the cows their flanks, trot about, and then stop, holding their heads high and still. Such displays got Black Bull rightly bothered. He is old with loose hide and drooping loins, but Black Bull is mighty, the biggest cow here and I reckon he's the biggest cow I've ever seen.

Black Bull crooks his neck to face Broken Eye Bull, horning at the ground and hoofing piles of dirt over his back. He snorts, then charges, and Broken Eye Bull runs away like a frightened calf. Then it's over just like that. None of them bulls seem keen on pushing Black Bull any further than they've done, and they move along one by one into the thickness of the herd. Black Bull lopes around his cows with his mammoth bullness swinging beneath his body. He changes directions and invites challenges from any of the other bulls, but none come. With his head high and tail straight back, Black Bull turns, and turns, and turns, and turns. He stops and waits with his front legs wide, shoulders hunched, and hooves dug into the dirt. He is the lead cow. From where I am I can see him plainly, but from where he is, I reckon he doesn't see me at all.

I turn my face away.

I stand when I hear a rustling coming from the other side of the oak.

"Anghf."

22

I look over the ledge of the hill. Another cow, a heifer, is coming up the far side. Her hooves slip on the stones as she makes her way up the slope. The cow turns her head for a moment, I figure to turn herself back, but then continues the climb. Her brown eyes move from the rocks, to the tree, then back to the rocks, and every step is slow and uncertain. I stare down the hill at her, but the cow pays me no mind, so I flick my ears and let the air out of my nose. Still she climbs.

"Anghf," she says again.

Her face is piglet pink; her creamy hide and head are patched with black. She has not milked yet, and given the width of her haunches, she hasn't birthed any calves either. When she reaches the crest of the hill, the smell of wet dandelion fills the air, and she moves past me.

"Unghf," I say, but the cow walks straight to the dead tree and sets herself underneath its twisting limbs. "Unghf," I say again, but the cow doesn't answer. I snort and lift my head updown, updown, updown, then shake it side to side terribly. I do this many times because I do not want her here, but she pays me no notice and instead just stares off over the cows to the far ends of the pasture.

I snort and walk to her front side so our eyes can see each other. I swing my head from side to side and snort once more.

The cow moves her head to peer around my body.

UpdownUpdownUpdownUpdown I move my head, and dig at the rocky soil with my front hoof. "Unghf!" I say. "Unghf!"

The cow does not answer.

"Unghf!" I say again, then lower my head and take three sharp steps toward her.

She flinches, I think.

"Unghf!" I say.

The cow turns her face toward the barn. I move myself to block her view.

"Leave now or I'll charge you right off this hill!"

"Anghf," she says after a pause.

"Unghf," I say, and the matter is settled.

I watch the cow make her way down the slope until she disappears into the others.

With night the cows fold their legs and slump down in the grass to sleep like dogs. I fight to not do the same and instead walk between the broads and the bulls, following fireflies through the darkness. For certain fireflies know nothing of fences or chewing grass or staying put. Fences don't figure for fireflies. They know nothing of this pasture business. They are simple, but they are free. If I had wings, Farmer Creely and his boy would see I don't belong here; I'd fly high above these cows and these fields and then I'd light my bottom.

My eyes dim in the dark. My hooves grow heavy, and my steps falter. I wish my knees would lock so I would not have to sleep in the grass. That's how horses do it. But cow legs tremble when they are tired and the ground pulls at our heads with such force, or so it seems. And nightly I go down like a dog, like the rest. But this night, like every night, I will try to stay on my legs. I close my eyes, my jaw slacks, and my thoughts drift to my mother's thick milk and the times my belly was so full of her, I thought I would burst. It's terrible to think, but I drank her even when I was not hungry.

"Anghf," she would softly rumble as I tongued at her teat.

When I had gotten my fill of milk, I would wait under her shoulders and nuzzle my nose into her face each time she bent to graze. Sometimes we'd stay that way for quite a while with her not chewing any grasses at all; other times I'd press my ear against her chest to listen to her inside. It always sounded like running horses.

For a cow, my mother was a sad type. No bull ever knew

her—or none of them came around anyways. I reckon having an ugly calf under her belly all the time rightly put some of those bulls off. But she was kindly about that, and she'd lay down close to me on cold nights to keep me warm.

By watching her I learned my grasses, and before long I'd grown too big to suckle. I would still try to drink her, bending my neck in such a way to get under her belly to her udder, but one day she went dry. After that I'd try to stay close, but she would prefer to eat grasses alone or rub her hide with the other cows. Calves are no use to cows beyond a certain point, that's my understanding of things, and I was my own cow then.

On occasion I'd see my mother following the herd to the stream or about the pasture, and I'd think it would be right and kind of her to come chew grasses with me. But she never minded me again. Last day I saw her she had grown so fat in the corral I hardly knew her face. I poked my head through the fence wires and called out to her as she walked along the chute.

"Unghf," I said.

She kept walking.

My legs can't hold me any longer, and my knees buckle into the grass. I slump to my side. At the end of each day, I am defeated in this way, and I lay my head down to sleep thinking how her milk tasted like apples.

Drops of rainwater wake me, and I stand to let the sky wash the scent of soil and grass from my hide. The other cows herd themselves into large groups to stay warm. Some of them lie back down on the wet grass while others stay standing with hides pressed onto hides. I stand alone and wait for puddles to form so I can drink.

I listen close. This is rain without thunder, the better kind of rain, and I lower my head and close my eyes. The weight of my body pushes my hooves deep into the mud. When my hide is soaked heavy, the water runs down my neck, behind my ears, over my face, and into the earth. I bend, I drink, and I quench my thirst.

After spending much of the morning in this way, I pull my hooves from the mud and I turn to the hill in the middle of the pastures. The same heifer is sitting under the tree.

"Unghf," I snort, and climb the hill.

The rain has not let up and I fall many times making my way up the slope. With each topple I slide and lose ground, but I press on. My legs are slow and my sides are thickly caked in mud by the time I reach the crest. I pause until my breathing no longer hurts and then walk myself to the cow.

She is nestled around the tree's trunk. Her hide is wet, darkened as the sky. I fury inside, and I think of telling her, *There is nothing on this hill for you, cow! Go eat grass, go drink from the stream, go lie with your kind! Go anywhere but here! This place is not for graceless creatures!*

I think of charging her from behind, goring my horns into the flesh of her rump and lifting it high into the air. I could trample her cowhead into the ground, shatter her ribs with ferocious kicks, or stand on her back and let the heft of my cowness slow her breathing to a stop.

"Anghf," she says.

"You don't belong here!"

"Anghf," she says.

She turns to see me, and I show her my broadside. I am large, I am dirty, and I am mean. *Don't take me on cow!* My spine tingles in the cool air. I lower my head, dig my front hooves into the ground, and turn my horns toward her. I snort. She turns away.

"Unghf!" I say.

She snorts, letting all the air out of her chest.

"Unghf!"

"Cow, look at me!"

When she turns to me again, I face her, swing my head and hunch my shoulders. I snort and horn the ground, tossing mud into the air.

She turns away. "Anghf," she says.

I charge, and slam my skull into the trunk of the oak. It rattles and snapping branches rain to the ground. This startles the heifer, but she doesn't get up. I back myself up and charge again. This time after I hit the oak, I dig my horns into its wood and slash at the trunk until it splinters. I do this again, and then I do it once more.

"Unghf," I say.

"Anghf," she answers.

I place my cowhead into her flank and push; she is soft and warm.

"Anghf," she says.

"Unghf," I say, pushing harder, but the cow is heavy like the oak and rooted into the ground. I lift my head.

The rain has turned white, swallowing the pasture and all the cows inside it. I lower my head again, and placing it against her haunches, I push. Her hooves cut into the mud and she pushes back. My head slides over her hind legs up to her belly, and I press my nose deep into her gut. To her chest and to her shoulders I push, snorting and twisting myself, but still the cow will not be moved. When I push on her neck, she wraps it around my face and presses her cheek against mine, and I pull back.

She looks at me and I flick my ears forward. I puff through my nose. I lower my head and nudge at her neck. The cow folds her face into mine again, and our hides rub.

"Unghf," I say, pulling away and I stare over the pasture.

The cow turns her face to do the same. All the pasture's fences have disappeared in the rain. I am cold, and my body quivers for warmth.

"Anghf," she says.

I lower my head and stroke my cheek along the length of her wet neck.

"Anghf," she says, folding around me again.

I try to pull back, but she wraps her chin behind one of my horns and holds me tighter. She cradles my face and my ears warm against her. My body shudders big, and that quiets the fine shaking for a while.

"Unghf," I say and lay down beside her. She pushes into me, rubbing her hide on mine, and we rest folded into each other under the oak until the rain stops.

When the clouds release the sun, we are warmed, and the pasture returns water to the sky in rolling columns of gray. The black flies swarm about our bodies, and the mosquitoes ring in our ears. And down on the pasture, beneath the cows, we watch as the earthworms surface, and the egrets walk on the mud to feast on them.

chaptêr four

The cows are nervous and hungry, standing with their backs arched, ears drawn down, and tails low. This is how such anxieties spread from cow to cow. Even the calves are still, huddling close to their mothers. I am nervous too, though I try not to show it. Standing beside My Cow from the hill, I snap my tail and kink it to show her that I'm not fearing what's going to happen. Then it happens.

The pasture gate swings open.

"Yah, yah, yah!" the men scream and race through the gate, jerking the reins of their horses.

"Neheheheh!" say the horses, and thudding hooves fill the air, ours and theirs.

The herd scatters in all sorts of ways. "Unghf," and "Anghf!" the cows say, splattering mud on each other's hides.

I say it too and run with them.

"Yah, yah, yah!"

The men crack long sticks over our hinds; the dogs come snarling.

"Owf, owf, owf, owf, owf, owf, owf!"

A bunch of us cows run as one; that's the safest way.

Going your own way around panicky cows will likely get you trampled. So I run this way, then that way, then this way again, and wherever the pack leads me. The men use their horses and their sticks to drive us one way, and then their dogs drive us back the other.

"Flash, come by!" one man shouts.

"Owf, owf, owf!" his dog says and half-circles around us. We turn.

"Hold," the man says, and the dog settles himself. The cows push out a bit.

"Flash, speak up!"

"OwfOwfOwfOwfOwf!"

"Walk up!"

The dog creeps closer to us, packing us cows back together.

"Unghf," and "anghf," we complain.

"Hold," the man says, and before we cows can even settle a bit, "In there!" he shouts. "Git in there, Flash!"

The dog lunges into the middle of the cow pack growling and snapping its jaws, cutting our pack in two. I turn to flee, but the dog catches me just above my rear hoof and bites.

"Unghf!" I cry, and kick my leg and run.

"OwfOwfOwfOwfOwf!"

"Yah, yah, yah!" the man says, cracking his stick over my shoulder when I stray outside the pack.

I turn, and I turn, and I run, and I run, and I see all the pasture cows being rounded up into smaller groups by other men with other dogs.

"Yah, yah, yah, cow!" The man cracks his stick against my side and it stings like hail. "Away, away!" he shouts to his dog, and the dog half-circles the other way around our pack. We turn again, and I am in the back.

"Hold!" the man says. His dog stills.

The man whispers to his horse, strokes its mane, then stands up in the saddle. He whistles to Farmer Creely.

"Hey, Farmer!"

"Yeah?" The farmer turns his horse and gallops close.

"Am I taking that big bull?"

Black Bull is standing alone in the middle of the pasture with his tail in his haunches and his ears drawn back flat against his head. The farmer stops his horse and looks.

"Yup," he says. "The big one goes to the production field."

The man waves his stick in the air, a signal to the farmer that he understands, and he sits back in the saddle.

"Flash, hold!" the man commands the dog. "Rexy! Mace! C'meer!" and two other dogs sprint over, grinning and barking. The man points his stick at Black Bull. "Go git! Go git!"

"Unghf," Black Bull says and he bolts—first this way,

then that way, and then this way again, with no sense at all as the dogs give chase. The dogs catch him near the fence by the chicken pen and they circle him over and over, until he turns around. The dogs bark much louder at Black Bull because he's bigger than the rest of us, and they menace him by nipping at his head and his heels. Black Bull runs straight for us with his horns in the air.

"Slow!" the man shouts. "Slow, Mace! Slow, Rexy!" and the dogs slow their charge. But Black Bull doesn't slow his charge, and he slams headfirst into our pack, sending a mess of cows to the ground and bucking his way to the safety of the middle.

"That'll do," the man says. "Yah, yah, yah," and he drives all us cows forward, with his three dogs taunting us until we reach the new pasture.

When the men, the horses, and the dogs leave, the cows eat and eat. The grass on the new pasture is thick and green, with wide patches lush with kale. The farmer wants this pasture eaten, so we will do just that. The cows swing their tails in excitement and gnash the crisp leaves between their teeth. But I cannot eat yet. I am missing My Cow.

The farmer and his men probably moved a few hundred broads and calves to this new pasture, but I count just two bulls: Black Bull and myself. Off in the corral, the men are herding cows left over from the last cattle drive. They are fat with healthy hides, and they eagerly walk down the curved chute until the corral is empty. But other cows are not so lucky. The men left some cows and bulls behind on the old pasture where the grasses have already been eaten. Cows wither on barren soil. For them, the coming days will bring uncommon hungers—bulls longing for their broads, the broads longing for their calves, calves longing for their mother's milk. Nothing lost is ever found in old pastures, and they will all have to endure until the new sprouts grow long.

"Unghf," I call out.

I have never known a cow the way bulls are supposed to know them. Most cows pay me no mind, and I reckon that's a factor. But it's also been hard to find a cow to my liking—some cows are just more equal than others. My Cow seems fine enough on all accounts. Besides I gather she has taken a shine to me.

I'm not big enough to see above all the cows. Instead I wander from cow to cow to find her, and after countless broads, I don't. Before long I am searching the same cows again. It is getting dark and soon they will put the sun

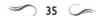

away. Without My Cow the night will be long and cold like before.

I call out again, and when she does not answer, I fear she was dog-chased to a different pasture.

At the gate the farmer has returned on horseback, but this time his boy rides in the saddle with him. The farmer stops the horse and starts counting us cows one by one, and he lowers his boy to the ground. The boy hangs from the top of the gate with both hands, swinging his legs forward and back as he sings. This is a song I know.

> *Frère Jacques*
> *Frère Jacques*
> *Dormez-vous? Dormez-vous?*
> *Sonnez les matines. Sonnez les matines.*
> *Ding, dong, ding.*
> *Ding, dong, ding.*

I walk closer to the gate to better hear the boy. I move my mouth and sing the words inside my head.

> *Frère Jacques*
> *Frère Jacques*
> *Dormez-vous? Dormez-vous?*
> *Sonnez les matines. Sonnez les matines.*
> *Ding, dong, ding.*

Ding, dong, ding.
"Sing with me."
Ding, dong, ding. Ding, dong, ding. *

"Anghf," I hear and I turn. My Cow is standing behind me, her mouth full of grass. And I wonder if she's been following me all along.

At the end of each day My Cow and I walk away from the remaining sunlight to the fence at the far end of the pasture. Here our shadows grow long across the grasses, up the fence post, and outside the pasture where the darkness eventually takes them. Each night we lay there in the grass with our hides touching, and we sleep until our shadows return with daybreak.

My belly is full of good grass and kale, but still I hunger. My Cow has stirred the bullness beneath me, making it feel full and firm. She is ready for calving; her

* For English translation see page 129.

hind is full, pink, and wet. I fight urges to climb on her back, not knowing how she'll react to that sort of thing. Black Bull knows My Cow is ready too. While we chew he snorts and trots by us with his horns high and tail straight out. He shows her his broadside and feeds nearby with one hoof off the ground. I chew, and I think, and I try to keep my ears off my head and my tail out of my haunches.

"Unghf," Black Bull says, and swings his head from side to side.

"Unghf," I answer and do the same.

My Cow is paying him no mind, and she follows me through the cows to chew elsewhere. When I lay down that night she is by my side and I dream about the dead oak, and its branches bursting with red leaves.

When I wake it is still dark, I am shivering, and My Cow is gone.

"Unghf," I call out.

I stand, and after my eyes adjust to the darkness, I weave my way through giant clusters of sleeping cows to find her. This time I do not walk quietly, and I wake many cows as I go. They cry out in protest, but it does not stop me.

It's easy to lose your senses among all the brush and broads lying about the new pasture. This much I know. If My Cow woke and wandered off in the night she'd be unlikely to find her way back to me before dawn. In the cold, she'd be right in bedding down with other cows, and I reckon I might even do the same on such a bitter night. If I find My Cow, and she is sleeping with other cows, I won't wake her. Instead I will lie with her, and I will lie with the others, until the sun is raised.

I call out to her again, and again.

"Anghf," I faintly hear My Cow calling from a bend in the fence. I flick my ears and snap my tail. Despite the darkness we have found each other.

"Anghf."

I walk to her.

"Unghf," I hear. She is with Black Bull.

I slow.

"Unghf," he says.

I am close.

They snort.

I stop.

I know what I will see when I turn the bend, and for a moment, I think about leaving them be. Cows will be cows, the farmer says, they don't know right from wrong or shit from sunshine. This I know to be true. But bulls will be bulls, and I am a bull—nothing less. So I decide to not leave them be. I decide to not let this be, and I charge around the bend, huffing and raising my horns.

"No! She is my cow!"

My Cow turns her face, but she does not startle at the sight of me. I fury at her for this. Black Bull approaches her from behind and climbs on her haunches, digging his front hooves into the hide on her back. She bends under the weight of his body and pushes her hind to him.

Black Bull steadies himself and tries to press his bullness into her.

I swing my head side to side. I hoof dirt over my back, "Don't!" and I horn the ground. I snort and take sharp steps toward them, then hoof and horn again. "I said she is My Cow!"

"Unghf," Black Bull says, paying me no mind. He cranes his neck to the night sky, and his eyes shine like the moonlight.

My Cow grunts.

"Unghf!" I cry out, and with my horns down low I charge. I charge at My Cow with all the speed and strength I have in my bull body, hoping to gore her belly wide open and spill her hateful insides all over this pasture.

My Cow scampers from underneath Black Bull, and he crashes to the ground with a fearsome groan. I chase My Cow, stabbing at her hind. When I cut into her rump she bleeds, and the red of her blood angers me more. I charge. She runs. When I tire I rest. She rests. Then I charge and she runs. I tire then I rest and she rests. I charge her and she runs. For the rest of the night and for most of the day, I charge and she runs.

Outside the back fence of the new pasture the land is thickly wooded with tall leafy trees. This is not pasture land. This is land no cow has ever known. I stare out and spread the fence wires apart with my horns. I want to crawl through, but I am not alone.

He is breathing heavily behind me, scraping at the dirt. I knew he would come for me. I slow my breathing and turn to face him.

"Unghf," Black Bull says. He horns the ground and shovels it over his back.

I think of running from him, I think of not running, I think of charging, and I think of not charging. He is a bull, and we will do what bulls have always done. This I know;

if I run from him now, I will run from him forever.

I lower my head.

"She is My Cow and you can never have her, Black Bull. Listen to me good! I am a bull too. I eat grass just like you do. I have horns just like you do. And I fury just like you do."

The powerful straps in his neck flex, swinging his massive head from side to side. He arches his back and hunches his shoulders. Nearby the broads and calves stop chewing and tuck their tails.

I show Black Bull my broadside, arch my back, and raise my horns. I snort. I turn my head to him again and dig my hooves under the grass into the ground. Updown, updown, updown I move my head and flip large chunks of pasture out of the earth with my horns. I am ready. Then there's a flash of light followed by blackness.

"Unghf!" I say. Cud spills out of my mouth, and my legs buckle with the force of the strike. Black Bull drives into me, pushing my haunches into the back fence, and I hear the fence post crack. We lock horns and he twists my head to the ground. I push back, but there is no moving him and my body bends upon itself.

"You can never have her, Black Bull!"

He pulls back, and I spring off the fence and slam my head into his. He catches my horns in his, and with a sharp twist of his neck, he tosses me off. When he comes at me again, I lower my head and steady my stance, but the impact rattles my spine, and my legs collapse under my body. Black Bull slams my head into the ground and thrusts my face into a mound of fresh dung. The whole weight of his body pins me there.

"She is My Cow! You can never have her!"

He snorts and pulls back. He rams me again, but I am still down and cannot get up. He lowers his horns and gores at my chest, cutting into my hide. I chop at his head with my hooves and kick at his body. His horns tear into my shoulder and my hind.

"Unghf," I say. "She is *my* cow."

He pulls away, and when I raise my head again, he charges. "My Cow."

When Black Bull strikes, the night sky bleeds into the day, and I let the darkness overrun my body.

The oak tree is alive and full of chickens. "Coohoo, coohoo, coohoo," they mock me from the branches. They peck at its wood, claw at its bark, and pluck its leaves. "Stop, you don't have any sense!" I say. I am too big to be a calf. In the distance, I hear the dogs snarling and it sounds like singing. I am slow and when they catch me they will chew on my hide like bones. Ding dong ding. Ding dong ding. The chickens pluck the oak bare, and when the leaves fall, the ants are frenzied, and they cut the weevils to pieces.

"Raise him."

I hear the men behind me. I turn my head. I know the faces. I know the men.

"Let's give him a good lift," the gun man says.

"He's done," one of the men say.

"It's over," says the other.

It is not over. I am not done.

"I reckon he's finished too, but let's give him a go anyways," the gun man answers.

The two men squat behind my back and haunch, and scoop their arms under my body. "One two three," and they try to lift me. I roll.

My legs are limp and my tattered hide soaks the good green grasses with blood. My flank feels like it is being gored again when they try to move me, and my head swings painfully on my neck.

"Have mercy on me."

"One two three lift!" one man says and both push again.

"Leave me be."

My cow legs are overcome with a terrible tremble, and I pull them with great shame under my body. I push up, but get only to my knees.

"Come on, big feller." The men push up from each side of me now, bracing their chests against my hind legs. "Up, git up," they say and push. "Git up!"

I fall back to my knees and lay my face on the grass at the gun man's feet.

The two men leave my side and stand far back from my body. "He ain't gonna go," one says.

"That's it," says the other.

The gun man sighs and points the rifle at my head. I close my eyes.

"Nothing sadder than a broken bull," he says, prying the metal mouth of the rifle under my cheek. "The sorriest of all animals. Don't you think?"

"Yup, sorry thing."

"Sorry thing."

The gun man presses the rifle over one of my eyes, and pushes it open. Then he lets it drop closed again. "Are you all broken, bull?" he asks, tapping the gun barrel against my horns. "You wanna git up?"

"Yes."

"Or you wanna die right here, bull? C'mon, now git yourself up."

I push up. My legs wobble then splay beneath me. I crash to the ground.

"C'mon, cow!" the gun man says stepping back. "Ain't you a bull? Ain't them horns on your head?"

I grunt and push again, swaying side to side until I am on my feet.

"Now raise those horns! Git 'em up!" he says.

I do, and open my eyes.

"That's it, boy!"

I steady.

"Cowboys—we have a bull!" the gun man cheers, and the men clap their hands. "Would you get a look at this broken and busted bull! Ain't he a smart lookin' animal?"

As soon as I set myself in my hooves, the gun man fires the rifle over my head. I shudder at the bang of it and fall to the ground. I scramble to get back up, splashing my own urine onto my belly.

All the men laugh.

"Yah, yah, yah," the gun man says and swats my hind hard with the rifle butt. "Yah, yah, yah," he shouts and swats again.

I run off, with my head low and my body covered with blades of grass in clotted blood.

The stream does not run through the new pasture, and I drink from a long trough of slow moving water. The silts swirl around my reflection, battering it, and I want it to carry me whole down the drain to the pipes that feed the kale. Black Bull is no longer agitated, but he is anxious, loping around his broads and snapping his tail. I will not survive another battle with him, this much I know. I would meet my death at the end of his horns or at the end of the gun man's rifle. From now on I must keep my head down, much lower than his. I must hang my head lower than his broads and even lower than some of the calves. I am the least cow here.

I stuff my mouth with kale leaves and chew slowly. The aphids jump in my mouth, and I crush them between my teeth and swallow.

My Cow has run off, and I scan the pasture for her creamy hide, but I do not see her. Defeated as I am, it would be wrong of me to charge her. She is her own cow now, and I must let her be.

I eat kale and then move along to the grass. The farmer wants this pasture field eaten and that is what us cows must do, eat and eat until all the green is gone. Though it pains me to walk so much, I eat and drink until I am fat

and slow. When the night comes, I wait for all the other cows to sleep. Then I walk to the back of the pasture, close to the woodlands, and surrender myself to the night by lying on the ground under some brush.

"Anghf."

I open my eyes, and when I raise my head, my horns rattle the brush above me. My Cow is standing so close to me I can smell her.

"Anghf," she calls out to me again. I rise and leave the brush. We are alone.

She turns her haunches toward me, and I see the three purple gashes where my horns tore into her hind. I lick them and savor her taste on my tongue. The bullness beneath me wakes and rises.

She snorts, and I nudge her neck. She folds it slowly toward me. She licks the base of my horns and the wounds around my ears. Stepping away, she faces the open pasture and shows me her hind. I smell her there and pull long breaths of her through my nose. She pushes her wetness into my face, and I lick.

"Anghf."

I flick my ears and snort. She pushes back. First I place one, then my two front hooves on her hind. My Cow pushes back. I can't hold her, and I slip off her hide and onto the ground. My Cow repositions herself, and I hoof at her haunches again. She pushes into me, and I climb onto her rump, with my chest pressing into her back. My bullness rages, and I clasp her sides tightly with my front legs and push into her. Each time I enter her, her cowness swallows me. A pleasure I have never known bursts inside me, and for a brief wondrous moment, I am standing on two legs like a man.

A calf flies into the sky; its body limp and its brown hide bloodied. It spins head over tail and thuds to the ground. The cows scatter. I stop chewing, so does My Cow, and we are still.

The calf is alive but its spine is kinked, broken. Its eyes scan the herd pleading for help but not one cow moves. Not even me. It wriggles on the grass like a snake but can't get anywhere. Black Bull pounces from a pack of broads, and with a fearsome snort, he drives one of his horns through the calf's chest and into the ground. The calf opens its mouth wide, its head trembling. Black Bull flexes his neck, flinging the calf over his shoulders. He bucks and turns, then drives his horns into the calf again, goring it on the ground. A single white cloud of breath floats out of the calf's throat and disappears. Black Bull tosses the calf again, lazily this time, and I am relieved when it lands, lifeless.

Black Bull sniffs the tiny body and pushes it with his nose. Its legs flop like rope. Black Bull raises his horns in the air, the dead calf at his hooves.

"Unghf," he says.

This was not Black Bull's calf and that's one good

reason he killed it. This was not my calf either; I surely don't know what I would have done if it was. Nothing I am could have stopped him. From the look of it, the calf must have belonged to Big Hump Bull, who was moved to another pasture in the last cattle drive. Good thing too because he would have been rightly bothered by Black Bull messing with one of his calves, and Black Bull would have killed them both. Now he'll never know what Black Bull did and maybe that's the best way.

Black Bull looks in our direction. I eat grass with my head low, eyes forward, ears down, tail still. He cranes his neck, and I step forward. When he's done looking and gone, I turn to My Cow—her belly is swollen, her haunches are wide. Soon she'll be calving.

Black Bull has not noticed her size yet, or at least I don't think he's seen her. He's been busy with the other broads and keeping the calves in line; his calves, I reckon. I try to keep us far away from him by chewing on opposite sides of the pasture, sometimes grazing in the dark and sleeping in the day. My Cow follows my lead, being the fine cow she is. But other times we come across Black Bull and there's no avoiding him. Those times I do my best to block his view, always situating my body between My Cow and him so he can't get a good look at her.

"We can't let him see you in this way. For certain he'd fury and kill the calf."

The nights get cold and the ground chills until the grass is sharp. I lay myself along My Cow, warming her hide until she falls asleep. All the cows are quiet, and I press my face against her belly to listen. When the calf inside wakes, it runs and tries to kick its way out of her gut, or so it seems. When it slows and sleeps I move my mouth, show my teeth, and sing one of the boy's songs.

> *Dodo, l'enfant do,*
> *l'enfant dormira bien vite,*
> *dodo, l'enfant do,*
> *l'enfant dormira bientôt.*
>
> *Une poule blanche,*
> *est là dans la grange.*
> *Qui va faire un petit coco*
> *pour l'enfant qui va faire dodo.*
>
> *Tout le monde est sage,*
> *dans le voisinage.*
> *Il est l'heure d'aller dormir,*
> *le sommeil va bientôt venir.* *

* For English translation see page 130.

The moon is sickled and sharp. The barn owls swoop and snatch mice from the grass to feed their young. I shut my eyes on this pasture, and in the morning one of the farmer's men will come on horseback, hook the dead calf with a long pole, and drag it across the grass and through the gate.

I wake. I know what must be done. I must find Black Bull before they raise the sun, and I must kill him while he sleeps. That is the only way; there may not be another time. In the remaining moonlight I walk and search for him among the hateful cows.

I figure spearing his neck with my horns over and over is the surest way. Better to keep my body on top of his so he can't get up, and I'll drive my hooves into his chest if he tries to rise. Should I not draw enough blood, Black Bull would be right in killing me, and I wouldn't fight him on it either. I'd expect nothing less from such a violently stupid animal. But if my legs hold and my strike is true, I can change everything. By morning I'd be the lead cow. My calf would be safe, and I'd likely have more calves with more cows in the coming seasons. I'd be right fine with that. As lead cow, all the other cows would look to me for proper chewing and proper drinking and proper bedding down. The greenest patches of pasture would be mine to chew, and all the other cows would fear my charge but battle to lie down near me and rub on my hide. Oh, how the notions light like fireflies in my head! Being lead cow would be like not being a cow at all!

In the distance Black Bull's hulking body rises out of the grass with each breath. I walk close, careful not to stir the other cows. He is surrounded by broads and calves, and I look for the best path to slay him. I step over a calf, one front leg then the other, one back leg then the other. I quiet my breathing and step between two broads, turn my whole body and walk around the head of another. I snake my way through a broad and a calf. I am close, with just a few cows between me and Black Bull's hind. I ready my neck; updown, updown, updown, then whip it side to side. I quiet myself and plan my approach to his throat.

Black Bull raises his head, facing the other way. I still myself and hold all the air in my chest. My ears flatten against my head and my tail drops. A throbbing takes over my body and with my hooves so close together I nearly topple. The air in my chest begins to burn and when I cannot hold it any longer I let it seep out of my nostrils. Black Bull turns and sees me standing above his cows.

Even in the dark he cannot mistake me; I'm the only

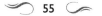

other cow on this pasture with horns on my head. He stares and I blink. I blink again and snap my tail. My head droops, and I turn it away from him. I survey the pasture, pretending like I'd somehow gone astray.

"How did I get so lost?"

Black Bull snorts but does not rise.

I lower my head further and turn it back to face him. His tail snaps. I pull my neck down as far as I can, and I chew on the grass around my hooves.

"Please, Black Bull, let me be. I am just a foolish cow, lost in my own pasture."

My neck is so buckled I cannot even swallow, and I chew like this until Black Bull is satisfied with my show of disgrace. When he is, I turn, and careful not to stir his cows, I walk off into the remaining darkness.

My Cow is calving, lying on her side in the kale looking sickly. She raises her head, bowing her neck to look at her swollen belly, and she then lays it back down again. Other cows notice this kind of thing, and I do my best to keep them away from her, even charging a broad or two. She's been up, down, up, and down again, all day long and still she cannot find comfort.

"Anghf," she says when the pains come.

Most cows like to be alone when they calve, but I cannot let My Cow be. She'd likely just set herself right there on the open pasture in plain view of all the other cows and wait for the calf to come. So when she's up, I prod her haunches, pushing her toward the back fence where the woods guard our backs and the brush hangs low over our heads.

"We must keep moving."

She tires easy, taking only a few steps before lying down again.

"Anghf," she says and slumps her head down.

"Be mindful, cow! We cannot stop here." But she never knows what I tell her.

Black Bull is chewing grass near the end of the water trough. He's paying us no mind. But there's no predicting the bull or the calf, this I know, and there is no telling how much time there is. I chew and I wait for My Cow to rise.

"Unghf," I say. "Here I am."

The ground has thawed, and the kale is dewy and crisp. Overhead starlings swirl in enormous black clouds until they settle on the farm's rooftops or perch themselves on the pasture's fences. Black Bull's calves have learned to use their legs, and they bound like grasshoppers around their mothers. The cold season is coming to an end, and soon the cicada nymphs will climb from the soil and warmer suns will turn them into jar flies.

My cow rises, I push my face on her rump, and we walk again.

My Cow is lying on her side again. Water pours from her hind; yellowed and milky, it settles into the soil.

"Anghf," she says, and her whole body wretches.

Blood comes, turning the ground frothy and pink, and I worry something is wrong. My Cow gasps and takes a full breath. She pushes and tenses and pushes again. Her hind widens like a mouth. When she pushes again, two small white hooves appear in her hind then go back in when she relaxes. My Cow breathes and presses again. The hooves return, followed by two thin legs stuck out straight. Her next push brings a nose, a head with ears and eyes, then shoulders, all covered in a slick coat of My Cow's insides. She rests. The calf's head is tucked tightly between its legs, and its eyes open and blink. My Cow pushes again, thrusting the body and haunches out from inside her. When the rear hooves come out, My Cow stirs and sits up, panting. The calf kicks and twists, tearing the greasy membrane from its head and hind quarters.

My Cow stands and inspects the calf. She licks its brown hide clean.

"Unghf," I say and walk closer. The calf lifts its head and flicks its ears. He is not ugly like me, but he is my calf, a bull calf.

Bull Calf's hide is smooth brown, save for the cream patch centered on his brow and snout. His ears are thin and shaped like lotus petals, and he slaps them over and over against his head. My Cow stands beside him eating her own insides, which had spilled out onto the grass.

The farmer and one of his men come on horseback. The man puts his horse between me and My Cow and Bull Calf, cutting me off from them. I bend my neck low to see. The farmer pulls close to Bull Calf, and after jumping from his horse, he grabs a towel and a box from his saddlebag.

"Easy does it, cow," he says. "Looks like you done a right fine job here."

My Cow raises her head, and showing no concerns, she returns to chewing her guts. Sometimes the farmer takes the calves from their mothers straight away; other times he leaves them be. I'd prefer it more so if the farmer leaves Bull Calf here on the pasture. That way I can see him grow horns and become his own bull.

The farmer kneels in the grass, rubs Bull Calf's body with the towel, and then scrubs down his haunches. "Let's see what we've got," he says straightening one of Bull Calf's hind legs and measuring it with tape. "Hip height about forty-two, maybe forty-one inches. Rump eighteen."

"Pretty big feller," the man on the horse says.

"Yeah, I 'spose he is," the farmer says. "Weight about seventy pounds. Hey, what's that bull doing?"

"Nothing, just looking it seems."

"Just keep an eye on him. Bulls ain't 'sposed to take such an interest in their young. I reckon it's a troubling sign."

"Maybe so."

"We don't need another dead calf on the pasture, especially another bull calf."

The farmer removes a needle from the box, draws liquid into it, and jabs it into Bull Calf's hind. Bull Calf's legs flail at the ground.

"This bull here," the man says tapping my flank with a stick, "he's tame, Farmer. You'll get no problems from him."

"A tame bull? Well, I surely prefer them that way."

"Well this one here sure looks tame enough."

"Let's hope he is. Bulls are bulls, nothing more, nothing less."

The farmer checks Bull Calf's hooves, then climbs back into the saddle. "That's it," he says. "Let's get moving."

When the man moves his horse from in front of me, Bull Calf thrusts his neck forward, pulls his knobby legs under his body, and pushes to stand. He trembles but rises. His tail snaps from side to side when he's fully up and then he bends his neck in such a way to drink the first milk from My Cow's teat.

A season passes. Black Bull has been no bother to us. Not sure why that is. He's likely seen Bull Calf with me and My Cow from far across the pasture; many times, I figure. But under these warmer suns, with all their rains falling, wild flowers and clover growing, he has paid us no mind. We chew mostly near the farthest pasture fences for good measure; there's nothing to be gained in troubling a predictably fierce animal. But I begin to think the old bull's senses are failing him.

In the early days, Bull Calf filled his belly with My Cow's milk. He grew tall and wide, and tufts of hair grew around the horn stubs on his head. Now, since her udder dried up, he bounces by my side and under my neck, walking where I walk, chewing as I chew. Good-to-eat mushrooms grow in the grass, bad-to-eat mushrooms grow in the dung; I show him this, and he learns right quick. Lavender flowers from the chicory brush sweeten on your tongue, and when snapped, tasty white milk oozes from the stems. I mix yellow grasses with green, and clover with kale to loosen the cud. When Bull Calf tires, he folds in the grass next to My Cow, and I venture deep into the middle of the pasture where I pack my mouth full of its greenest kale. I carry the leaves back, denying myself from chewing, and lay them under his mouth. He delights in eating that way, and I go get him some more.

Like the other cows there's no talking to Bull Calf—try as I might. I say "unghf," My Cow says, "anghf," he says "mneweh," and so it goes. By season's turn he'll be bucking and charging like a bull though, and My Cow will be ready for calving again.

"Giddyap."

The farmer rides his horse on the soil path between this pasture and the last, leading a pony by its reins. The farmer's boy follows too, skipping and singing alongside the pony. I move to chew near the fence and Bull Calf follows me, being the fine calf he is.

"Look at my Bull Calf. Teach him to sing."

Bull Calf stretches under me and pokes his head through the fence to watch the farmer and his boy.

"Unghf," I say, but they don't stop or even much notice us, and the shame scorches my ears, and burns in my jowls. Bull Calf does not notice this, or so it seems, and we watch them as they walk off.

Far down the trail, they turn to the trotting fields where their horses can run without concern for fences and pens. We chew again. I sing inside my cowhead, and I imagine it is not me singing, but Bull Calf singing, and the song is so grand it makes the boy turn around, come back, and sit by the fence to listen.

The cows swarm around the pasture like angered yellow jackets. There's no telling what set them off, but when the raging horde comes close to us, I stop chewing, plant my hooves in the grass, and shake my head side to side. My Cow tucks her tail and moves behind me; Bull Calf steps up close to see best.

The cows come hoofing and swirling, many of them at once, charging all about. I lower my head and horn at the ground, but still they come. I charge, parting the cows, and they circle around us. My Cow tries to outrun the pack, as cows are known to do, but she disappears into the herd. I guard Bull Calf, running round and round him. He is shaking, so I push my hide into his, and I slam my body against the other cows when they come too close. I turn this way, I turn that way, and I turn every way around Bull Calf, warning cows that my deadliest strike is ready should they decide to challenge me.

"Anghf," and "anghf," the cows cry.

"Unghf," I say.

"Unghf," I hear. It's Black Bull, running just like the rest.

Black Bull barrels into me, knocking me and Bull Calf to the ground. I scramble back up, but Bull Calf is slower to rise. Black Bull bucks his way into the horde, then all the cows slow their charging, grouping themselves by the back fence. They press hide-to-hide. I press my hide onto Bull Calf, and he has stopped shaking. I snap my tail and lower my horns when Black Bull steps forward.

"This is Bull Calf, my calf, and you can never have him!"

I horn at the ground and shovel grass between my legs with my hoof. Updown, updown, updown, I move my head with more ferocity than I ever have before. I hunch my shoulders. Black Bull snorts and shakes his head from side to side, but keeps his horns high.

I snort, and shake my head again. "Unghf," I say. "You are a vile beast. I am ready to kill and I am ready to die."

Nothing.

"Back down, Black Bull!"

But Black Bull stares over us, paying me and Bull Calf no mind. He flicks his ears then draws them flat to his head. The hair along his spine rises and his tail snaps stiffly from side to side. I turn and Bull Calf does the same. At the gate of the old pasture where the grasses have grown back thin, a line of trucks packed with cows waits to be unloaded.

Some of the new cows charge the old cows when they first come off the trucks, but the fury doesn't last. Cow after cow spills down the chutes. Before long, the old pasture is filled to the fences with all sorts of unfortunates—old broads with sagging hides and swinging udders, black heifers, bulls with no horns, even some cows with horns, and lame calves limping close behind their mothers. None of the new cows are plump, their hips pointy and sharp. When the last of the trucks finally pulls away from the pasture, the cows stand rooted like trees to the ground, tails still and flicking their ears with uneasy calm.

Some of the cows along the edges look across to our pasture where the kale leaves crunch beneath our hooves.

"Anghf," they say.

I turn away and lead My Cow and Bull Calf around some brush where the longing will have a harder time finding us.

After chewing most of the day, I am thirsty and Bull Calf follows me to drink from the trough. Our reflections eddy together in the water then separate. Two cows look up from the surface, a bull and his calf. For the first time, I notice

Bull Calf's eyeballs jut from his head in the same way mine do. His snout and brow are a different color, that's plain to see, but they have the same shape as mine and his nose is turning dark. Our heads have a similar shape only his is smaller. Bull Calf stops drinking and I watch him as the ripples settle in the water. He looks, flicks his ears, and in that moment I think he sees me, or perhaps sees himself. I open my mouth to tell him my name, but before I can get it out of my throat, he drinks again.

When night comes My Cow, Bull Calf, and all the other cows sleep, but I cannot. In the dark I wander and listen to the new cows cry out. Each cow has a different hunger, and I've weathered each one the same. They are simple hungers for simple appetites. But none of these cows hunger like I hunger, I think. I am the leafy field and I am the thorns on the brush. I am the pasture inside the pasture, and the only cow here truly starving.

They bring the sun up under the clouds just as most cows are starting to rise. The chickens are bothered this morning and that makes the cows stir early. The gate squeals open.

"Yah, yah, yah!"

And the dogs race in again. Bull Calf doesn't know what to make of this and he steps close to me, frightened, as all the cows begin to run. Then we run. He and My Cow stay close, and I lead them to the middle of the stampede. I reckon it's the safest place to keep us together.

"Git in there, Mace. Git in there!"

"Neheheheh," the horse says.

One dog runs into the cows barking and nipping, cutting our pack in two. We run with the larger group and two of the farmer's men drive the smaller pack away with their sticks and their dogs. I run this way, then that way, then this way again, and My Cow and Bull Calf stay close behind.

"Hold up, Mace. Walk up."

The cows pack tight around us.

"Speak up."

"Away, away!"

The cows shift.

"Yah, cow, yah!" The man cracks his stick on the rump of a stray broad and uses his horse to drive her back into the pack. She has a head thick and uneven like a boulder.

"Anghf," she says.

"Unghf," Black Bull says from the front.

"Hold, Mace."

Another man on horseback rides over with a black-and-white dog jogging behind.

"Farmer says the old black bull goes to the corral, the other bull stays put."

Both men search the cows and find my horns. I lower my head. I've had enough of this pasture life, I figure, and I've got to get Bull Calf and My Cow to the corral where we can all get fat on the farmer's feed—even if it means chewing grass in the very shadow of Black Bull.

"Gotcha. You here to help?"

"Yup."

"Jessie, come by."

And one dog circles us.

"Mace, away, away."

The other dog circles us in the opposite direction.

"Hold up. Walk up."

The dogs creep in and the cows pack tight.

"Speak up."

"Owf, owf, owf, owf, owf!"

"In there! Git in there!"

The dogs race into the cows and cut the pack in two again. Through the rumbling cow legs, I follow Black Bull's hooves best I can. He runs this way, then that way, and I do the same, following him with my head low and horns forward.

"Yah, cows, yah! Yah!"

Black Bull turns, and I turn. He runs, and I run. I turn and run so much I lose my senses in all the cows, and I lose him in the dust. But then I find him again when the cows stop and the dust settles around their hooves.

"Hold, Mace."

I breathe heavy and my tongue is thick and dry. The cows pack hide to hide. In the distance I hear other cows being driven away. Black Bull's hooves shift from side to side, several cows in front of me. Between my own legs I can see My Cow's hooves behind me. I keep my head down and wait.

"Flash, c'meer."

Another dog runs over.

"Come by, Flash. Away, away, Mace."

And the dogs circle us.

I hear the crack of a stick on cowhide, then the man shouts, "Yah, yah, yah! Let's move cows. Let's moooove."

And with my neck bent to the ground, I walk with the herd to the corral.

"Coohoo, coohoo, coohoo," the chickens call when we are driven in. Ahead of us, the bale wagon dumps giant spools of hay on the corral grounds. After rolling them out, the men pluck them apart with pitchforks. This is very good hay—different leaves mixed with brown grass, blanketing the ground. The cows kick it up as they walk, and I draw huge breaths of rye and alfalfa into my chest. I snatch a mouthful, chew it, and savor the taste on the back of my tongue. It is delicious. Once the men and the dogs leave us, the gate clanks closed and I lift my head, but not all the way, and I turn. My Cow has stopped behind me to sample the hay too, but Bull Calf is gone.

"Where is our calf?"

The herd thins, spreading across the corral grasses and My Cow keeps chewing. I scan the cows for his brown hide and creamed snout but cannot find him. I walk and My Cow follows.

"Unghf," I call out over and over, listening for his call, but he does not answer.

Soon I realize Bull Calf is not here. There is not a single calf inside the corral fences. I figure the men must have had him dog-chased to another pasture or just kept him on the production pasture. My legs fold beneath the weight of me. Those damn ugly dogs. I could have stopped this and turned on them. I should have let Bull Calf run in front of me where I could've kept my eyes on him. I should have planted my hooves in the ground and gored each and every one of those dogs with my horns. He's not even his own cow yet. I worry I haven't taught him enough of what I know. Sure he knows his grasses, and I reckon that's the most important thing, but he's still no bull, and he won't know how to 'fend himself. I rise and stick my head through the fence. I get a good look at the cows on the first pasture, but the production pasture is too far down across the trail for me to see.

"Anghf," My Cow says.

"Unghf," I tell her. "He's not here."

During the day I chew grass and hay near My Cow, trying my best to keep my head low so the men don't see the horns on my head. I feed at the farmer's trough only at night for the same reason. The feed is wondrous. In the moonlight, it looks like oats, but it tastes like every grass and flower I have ever known. When I have my fill, I walk back to My Cow with my belly stretched, and I fall to the ground, landing softly in the hay beside her. My mind always takes me back to Bull Calf, and I wonder if he's grown any more like me.

The months pass in this way and soon cold air slinks across the farm.

"Jacques?"

"Yeah, Paw?"

"I'll be by the hogs."

"'K, Paw."

"Now you stay right there by the chickens."

"I will, Paw."

The boy nods and sits on the ground. His jacket bunches around his neck. He pokes a stick through the chicken wire and sings to them even as he taunts them.

Alouette, gentille Alouette

Alouette—je te plumerai

Alouette, gentille Alouette

Alouette—je te plumerai

The bale wagon has not come and almost all the hay has been eaten off the ground. Thin blades of grass poke through the dirt and are coated with frost. I am fat and slow, and still I am cold. I press my hide into My Cow, she presses back into mine, and her skin is soft and warm. She has fattened too, her face is puffed and pink, and her haunches have widened like the other broads in the corral. I pull grass and the blades snap, leaving their roots underground. I tongue the soil for seeds and pick them in my teeth and bite.

Black Bull is bigger than ever, having spent most days hunched over the feed trough with his broads. On occasion he charges a cow away from the feed or from a good pile of hay, but as he grew larger, his ferocity waned and now few cows pay him any mind.

One of the dogs has whelped, and she is lying on her side surrounded by her litter just outside the chicken pen. The farmer's boy tends to her pups.

The farmer approaches the corral with some of his men, and as usual I lower my head to hide my horns. Two of the men have rifles slung up on their shoulders, one carries an electric prod and the rest carry whipping sticks.

They walk along the length of the chute, pulling on the rails and fixing it in place. When they reach the corral, one of the men straddles the door to the chute like he's riding horseback and slides it wide open. The farmer and the rest of the men enter the corral.

"Coohoo, coohoo, coohoo!"

The chickens have seen this happen before, and I have too, several times, and my body shakes with excitement. I turn to My Cow, who I reckon has no idea where that chute leads.

"We did it, My Cow! We are leaving the pasture! We will never see these men or their wretched dogs ever again, I know this much. Surely I'll miss the boy, but beyond the birch-wood building, there may be many more boys singing. I'd make them all sing to me at once, and I would do my best to sing along with them. Don't you understand what a glorious day this is, My Cow? If you would listen to me just this once, I would tell you stories about all the cows I've seen walk this pass before. Fat cows, stately cows, calm cows walking along the chute with their tails in the air and their heads high. You see, there is no grass in the chute so there's no reason for chewing. That's simple cow business. Let's forget we ever did that! When cows are in the chute, there's no need to act like cows at all. Don't you understand that? There's no bucking or charging, no horning or hoofing in the chute. I'm telling you the truth; for them, pasture life is over. The cows walk with refinement. They walk with the grace of man. They walk with redemption—knowing all their suffering through frost and famine has gotten them to this very point. You know, I've never seen one of them look back on these pastures, not even my own mother. I wouldn't lie to you about that, My Cow. I called to her from the pasture fence, but she kept on walking. Such is the world waiting for us, so wondrous it can even make a broad dismiss her own calf!"

My Cow swallows her cud as the men come close, cracking their sticks against cow hinds, herding us together. I lower my horns and make sure to keep cows on all sides of me. I surely don't want the men finding me now—not when I'm so close to leaving. My Cow follows me, and the cows pack more tightly around us as we gather around the mouth of the chute.

"Yah, cow, yah," the men say. "Move along, cows, move along."

"I'm off," the farmer says. "I'll be in Markettown until late. Once you get half these cattle cleared into the chute you can shut it down. We'll bring in the next half in the morning."

"Right, Farmer."

"Right it is," says the farmer, walking off.

"Yah, yah, yah, cows, move along, move along, move along."

The mouth of the chute is several cows wide, and it's easy to hide my head under the haunches of the cows in front of me. If the men on the railings see me now, they'd surely move me back to the pastures.

"Anghf," My Cow says, and I let her in behind me. We walk. The chute narrows and turns, narrows and turns again. Soon it's just three cows wide, then just two, then just one. I'm in, and I follow the cow in front of me. The chute curves between the road and the old pasture—between the life I've only known and the life I have never known. As we get closer to the birch-wood building, the chute curves more sharply, like the body of a giant snake. The line slows, and I stop.

I look through the railings and watch the cows in the old pasture chewing in the same corners of grass I once chewed on and calves scampering by their mothers on un-certain legs. I fed on those grasses and so did my mother. The oak tree where I first saw My Cow rises out of the hill like tremendous horns, and I recall a rainy day. I look to the production field in the distance and see a few cows grazing on its green grasses. A bull, maybe even Bull Calf, paces the closest fence. I close my eyes and carry kale to him once more and lay it under his snout.

"May the pasture make you strong, Bull Calf."

My Cow pushes her face into my haunches. The cows behind her are pushing against her rear and they begin to buck. The chute rattles. This is not supposed to happen. My Cow bucks behind me, ramming me forward and into the shadow of the birch-wood building. As I follow the rump of the cow in front of me, the walls close in. The chute dims without the sunlight, and it turns so sharply, the cow in front of me disappears around the bends—

"Anghf," I hear, then *Clank, clank, thrisht!* followed by scrambling hooves. *Clank, clank, thrisht!* I hear again.

"Anghf."

Inside the building, it smells like manure and blood, and the chute becomes so narrow my sides rub the walls when I walk. I cannot turn my body. Behind me, the cows heave forward again and shove me around another bend. The cow in front of me enters a stall barely wide enough to fit her haunches and then a solid gate closes behind her.

Clank, clank, thrisht! I hear the cow's hooves thrash against the metal door, and it seems like they will never stop. Then there's a *Phthwot! Phthwot!* and they stop.

When the stall gate opens again, I step in.

The stall is dark but has a hole for my head. I poke my face through it.

Clank, clank, thrisht!

Iron braces close around my neck and pinch my skin. I jerk and try to pull my head out, but the braces are too tight. My knees slam against the front wall, and I kick at the metal gate behind me with both of my hooves. "Unghf!" I cry. The floor sinks below me and a cold steel shaft holds my body off the ground. The room is so bright it blinds me. When my eyes adjust, I see life draining from the cow in front of me. She is dangling upside down by one of her rear hooves. There is a hole in the center of the cow's head—right between her eyes—and her throat has been slit clear across. Blood pours out of her neck and splashes on the floor.

"Hold up, hold up, hold up!" shouts a man on a platform over my head. "Shut it down!" The man is wearing a white coat, long yellow rubber gloves, a visor, and a mask. He pulls his mask down. "I said shut it down!"

A bell rings and the commotion stops.

Ding, dong, ding, ding, dong, ding.

I cannot breathe. There are many dead cows in the building—some of them headless, some of them skinned, and all of them hanging. Piles of cow parts and entrails sit on blood-drenched metal tables. Dozens of men in blood-splattered white uniforms surround each of them with saws, knives, and giant claspers.

"We got a bull here! Hey foreman, we got a bull here!"

The foreman walks over on the catwalk and checks the clipboard in his hands. "The schedule says there's supposed to be a bull processed today."

"Not this bull! Not this bull," the man says, flailing his hands. "The old black bull!"

"The black bull's in the chute?"

"Yeah."

"What does Farmer want with this bull here? Ain't he too ugly to sire?"

"Nope. Already has."

"Well I'll be damned."

"Plus this one's younger and he's tame," the man says. "Farmer prefers the bulls to be tame."

"How'd he get in the corral?"

"Don't know, sir. He was supposed to be on production."

"Okay then, let's get him out of there. Get him back where he belongs. Put him in the parlor 'til Farmer gets back."

"Will do," the man above my head says and pulls his mask back up. "Can I get some help with these horns?"

Another man walks over holding a mechanical saw. It screams when he presses the trigger and my whole head clatters when it cuts. One horn falls, then the other. The man picks them up and tosses my horns to the floor.

"Okay, let's get him out."

The floor rises below my feet again, and I try to run but can't. My legs are heavy and my knees are weak. The side of the stall opens and the men prod me with an electric pole. My body leaps and twitches. They prod me again, and again, and push me to the holding parlor. From here I can see everything.

The man punches a button on the wall, gears churn, and the line of hanging cows starts moving again. My Cow's head pops up through the opening in the stall.

Clank, clank, thrisht! And her head is caught.

I open my mouth. "My Cow!" I try to shout. "No! Get out! Run!" I move my lips. "I'm here!" I try to push the air through my throat. I buck against the walls. "I'm sorry. I'm sorry! I'm sorry!" I scream, but the words are trapped inside my body.

The man who sawed off my horns places a large pipe between her eyes, *Phthwot! Phthwot!* My Cow jerks and she is stunned, nearly limp. The side of the stall falls open. A mechanical arm sweeps a chain around her hind hoof and pulls her out hanging upside down. She thrashes her free hind leg and arches her neck. The next man on the processing line wraps his arm tightly around her muzzle and slices into her throat with a long steel knife. Her soft cow skin cuts easily. She jerks and kicks again, but as the blood pumps from her neck down her jaws and to the floor, the kicking becomes slow, weak, and then it stops. The overhead conveyer swings My Cow's carcass raining a river of blood to the next station.

Phthwot! Phthwot!

Another cow is already dangling and having her throat slit. It all happens so quickly.

A man with a chainsaw saws off My Cow's head. A plume of blood and flesh jets from the sides of the saw when he cuts and some parts of My Cow land on the floor by my hooves. Once her head is taken clear off, it is placed on a metal table where men inspect it. A man with a short blade cuts at the corners of My Cow's mouth giving her a ghastly smile. He spreads her jaws, reaches in her throat and with a quick slice of the knife, he yanks out her tongue and tosses it into a large bin with other tongues. He slices off her lips, exposing all her brown teeth and throws them onto a conveyer belt. The hide of her face is torn off and then her cheeks are cut loose and tossed onto the conveyer too. Once her face is fully stripped, her head with its hanging hide is hung on a travelling hook and carried away.

My Cow's headless body lurches down the line—one man cuts off both her forelegs; the other man is on a raised platform and he cuts off her free hind hoof. The men cut around My Cow's hind and seal it with wire coil. Her body swings over to men holding skinning knives. One man makes a long fine cut along her belly while the other slices along her spine. Then circling in opposite directions, they peel her cow skin away, exposing her red and yellowed insides. The men remove small strips of hide from her legs and haunches and toss them into a bin, but the large sheets are handed to another man who hoses them off with water before stacking them neatly.

Her carcass spins on the trolley, and her belly is carved wide open. Two men slice out her guts and spread them on a table. My Cow is left empty inside and her chest gapes at me like an open mouth.

"I didn't know," I tell her.

Bits and pieces of her are thrown away along with her entrails and hind parts, but some of her larger insides are placed in baskets and carted away.

With her insides fully taken out, My Cow's body sways more freely and hooks are placed in both of her hind legs. A man removes the chain from around her rear leg and saws off her remaining hoof. With two more swift cuts of his saw, what remains of My Cow is spilt into three large pieces; her two sides are left hanging on hooks and her spine crashes to the floor on top of many others. Two men reach for her flanks and lift them off the hooks. They place them on tables and blast off bits of flesh, hair, and hide from each with a jet of water. Then her shoulders and haunches are hacked off with cleavers and the meat is carved from her bones with long thin knives.

I try to buck out of the parlor, but the sides are too close for me to gather any force. "Unghf!" I say and hope the others hear me.

Different cows die in different ways. Sometimes the stunning pipe kills them flat out, and they never see it coming. Those are the lucky cows. But other times the pipe doesn't work proper and the cow is hung upside down still alive and frantic. Those cows have the most horrible deaths because the bloodletter slashes at their necks with such a panicked ferocity he often doesn't get the cut right on the first try. The cows flail and kick at him but in the end it never really matters much; the bloodletter always gets the job done.

Black Bull pokes his head through the opening in the stall. The braces close around his neck. He doesn't fight at all. The men cut off his horns, blast a hole in his head, swing him upside down, slit his throat, rip his skin off, chop off his hooves, hollow him out, and then carve him into tiny pieces. The savagery overwhelms me. I collapse against the sides of the parlor stall, my head striking the steel railings and smearing them in blood.

I am a calf but I am huge. The other cows crawl under my hooves, swarming like ants. They storm up my legs, bite at my flesh, and chew the hairs from my hide. They taste my enormity. To them I am incomprehensible and after a while they leave me be. "The pigs come first," the farmer says, and I wonder whatever will become of them.

A shock quakes my body.

"Git up, bull. Time to go."

I open my eyes. The farmer and two of his men are at the parlor gate striking the rails with poles. Another shock from the prod—then comes another. The dead cows are gone.

"Let's go, bull. Time to go. Back to pasture with you."

"Just get me out of here. Take me anywhere but don't leave me here."

"C'mon, bull, to yer feet."

I rise and they open the gate.

"Looks like you had a rough day, bull. Let's get you back where you belong."

"You're going to be tame now, ain't you?"

"Unghf," I say. "I'm tame."

"'K, now," the farmer says and fits a steel collar around my neck.

Outside the birch-wood building, the men climb on horses. They have already put the sun down and the farm is dark and quiet. The farmer and one of his men ride their horses aside me, the other man rides behind. The dogs trail us all, panting. When I stop, the men shock me with the prod. So I don't stop. The men talk.

"You know in some places the cow is considered sacred," the farmer says, "the best of all animals."

"Imagine that."

"Hard to believe, I know," the farmer says, and after a long pause, "India, I think it is. They say cows protect the children and in turn the gods protect the cows."

"Is that right?"

"Well, I'm not sure how right any of this is. I'm no Indian. But they say cows give them milk, plow their fields, and fertilize their lands. Even the dung is used as fuel over there in India, I think—burning cow dung keeps the skeeters and evil spirits away, so they say."

"Ever tried it?"

"Reckon I haven't," the farmer chuckles. "So I 'spose we got plenty of both around here."

The men laugh.

I used to wonder why men hid their skins under hats and clothing. I always figured they were just ashamed of their uneven wiry patches of hair, or their lack of tails on their hinds, or lack of horns on their heads. But now I know better—it's the blood.

We turn at the chicken pen, and they are cooing softly. It is true chickens are born with wings that will never fly, but now I see cows are much lower animals—born with legs that can't outrun dogs, eyes that don't weep, and a mouth that doesn't shout, but only eats.

I arrive at the production pasture. They open the gate, remove my collar, and push me in. All the cows are sleeping.

chapter nine

Imust find Bull Calf and I must get him out of here. I will not stop until I do. I would even go back to slaughter if I thought it would spare him the knife. I crisscross the grass and kale in the production pasture searching for Bull Calf in the dark.

The pasture is more crowded than it used to be with hundreds of cows lying hide to hide in big clusters. Many of them are packed so tight I can't even tell where one cow ends and the other begins. I'm careful not to rouse them, teetering between hooves and heads. I am slow to move with my added age and fat, and I'm never sure which cows I checked and which cows I didn't. I'm not even certain I'd recognize Bull Calf if I did see him—calves change so much with the seasons. I reckon Bull Calf's grown big by now with broad shoulders and horns on his head. My legs tremble when I walk and I can do nothing to still them.

I call out to him in the dark and a brown bull raises his head. I keep walking.

It's too cold for fireflies and only the half-moon lights my way. My shadow is faint, but it crawls along the grass and up the flank of a heifer. There on her side I see my head without horns and I turn away.

I call out again and a few cows stir, then I call out louder, "Unghf! Unghf! Unghf!" and I wake many of them. They flick their ears at me, snap their tails, and lift their heads. None of them can make any sense out of me. My appearance must be making them anxious; a hornless fattened old bull wandering the pasture in the night. I walk off.

Under the brush by the back fence, not far from where My Cow gave birth to him, I find Bull Calf sleeping alone. He's grown some and his horns have started to lengthen. His nose has blackened like mine and the cream patch on his brow and snout has turned brown as clay, but still I knew him right away.

"I will get you out of here, Bull Calf."

I fold my legs and quietly lower myself to the grass. He stirs but doesn't wake. "Unghf," I tell him and softly lay my neck over his.

Bull Calf startles and springs to his legs. It is morning. The sun is still low in the sky and has yet to warm the air above the grasses. Bull Calf plants his hooves wide in the dirt, hunches his shoulders, and horns at the ground. "Unghf," he says, "unghf."

I rise too. "Remember my face. I sired you. I fathered you. I fed you."

Bull Calf scratches at the ground with his hooves. Up-down, updown, updown, he shakes his head. The hairs stand up along his spine and he shows me his broadside, then he faces me again and horns at the ground.

I lower my head to show him I have no horns.

He snorts and charges, but he's not big enough to harm me. I stand my ground and let his body slam into me. He grunts on the impact and charges me again. I lower my head and he batters into my skull—over and over again—until his legs give way and my hide has been gashed. When he tires, he folds himself back in the grass with his tongue hanging limply out of the side of his mouth.

"Bull Calf, follow me." I turn to lead him.

Nothing.

"I cannot let them kill you here. That is what they plan to do. I will never leave your side again."

Nothing.

"Please, Bull Calf. I've seen the horror of this farm. The men will butcher you. The dogs are kind compared to the men. The men will tear off your hide. They will saw off your head, and they will cut out your tongue. I could not live if you were killed here. You must live, I must live, and we must leave. You have to follow me."

I walk off, but Bull Calf does not follow. I turn.

"Come now."

He snorts but does not answer me. I leave the brush and walk off into the pasture. Far off by the corral I hear the farmer and his men fixing the chute in place, clanking on its rails, making sure it's set. Today's kill will soon be underway, and I wouldn't know how to stop it if I could. The bloodletter is waiting for me and Bull Calf too, this much I know, unless we break from these fences.

A lone white egret walks the grass in my shadow. The egrets fly in and fly out of the pasture as they please and until now I never saw the sense in it. Why would they choose to walk under cows if they could soar in the sky, I'd ask myself. Now I know they don't come here for us cows. They come here for the worms. We cows feed on the grass and uproot the worms from their homes. The egrets feed on the worms. Most cows don't know their chewing even figures in the deaths of worms—or the lives of egrets, but it does.

I bend my neck and snatch kale in my teeth. The leaves I once devoured taste sour in my mouth, but I still pack my cheeks as full as I can. The gate of the corral slides open; I'd know the sound anywhere. The farmer's men shout yah yah, and I know the remaining cows in the corral are being funneled to their deaths.

I walk back to the brush where Bull Calf is still folded on the grass with his head up and ears flicking. I move close to him and he snorts. He snaps his tail. I stop. When he turns his head aside, I walk to him again. I lower my head.

He snorts again.

I open my mouth and let the kale spill out, dropping all the leaves under his face. He shakes his head sharp and then turns and sees my face.

"Unghf," he says.

"Yes," I say. "Unghf."

chaptêr ten

After the cows have warmed under the sun, they roam the pasture eating its grasses and drinking from the trough. They do this with such constancy and commitment I am overcome by the senselessness of it all. Cows fattened by grasses, kale, and the farmer's feed are slaughtered without mercy. By their own doing, the cows could just not eat at all and starve themselves—but none of them ever do. Such is the allure of ignorance over agony. I turn to Bull Calf behind me. He is chewing and I chew too. Cows eat grass, and I reckon this is how it has always been.

I call out to Bull Calf, and he follows me to the back fence. The woods outside are dense with purple ash and flowering red dogwoods, and the branches rise and weave together to block out the sun. On the ground the uneven grasses are knotted by bramble and nightshade, and it's hard to figure the sort of animal that can walk through it all. I poke my snout between the fence wires. With no horns on my head, it slides easily through. I breathe the woods. I place my front hoof on the lower wire and push down with all the bull strength I have. I arch my neck, pushing up on the top wire with my skull. My hoof slips, and I try again. The top wire cuts into my hide, but I press harder and the wires pry apart, just a little. I step back, then pry them apart again. The wires are tight, but suddenly there's a snap and the bottom wire loosens. A hole is made, but it's still not big enough for Bull Calf to squeeze through, let alone me. I brace the top wire against the stubs of my horns. I place one hoof, then the other hoof on the bottom wire. It sways forward and back under the weight of my body, but it doesn't break or come loose from the fence post. I push up with my head and the wire rasps into my flesh. Blood trickles down my snout and drips on my tongue. I push again, then there is a *plink* and the top wire loosens. I step off. Now the hole is certainly large enough for Bull Calf but not me. I turn to him.

"Bull Calf, you have to leave here now."

The cows behind us are stirring, agitated. They cry, but I do not turn.

"Bull Calf, you must leave here now!"

Bull Calf does not answer me. "I won't let the men butcher you. Once you are through the fence, I will make the hole bigger, and I will follow you. I will follow you from this pasture! But you must leave here now, before it is too late."

"Unghf," more cows cry.

"Bull Calf, go!"

Bull Calf still doesn't go, so I walk behind him and push on his haunches with my head. He pushes back. "Move, Bull Calf, move!" Still he fights me. "You don't have any sense about this place!" With his front hooves locked straight and his hind bucking, I slide his body across the grass to the hole in the fence. I hunch my shoulders and give him the hardest push I have, but Bull Calf braces his hoof on the bottom wire and pushes back.

He grunts and won't go.

I stop. The cows are still crying and milling about the water trough. Their backs are arched, their ears are flat to their heads, and hardly a cow is chewing. Bull Calf jogs around me and lopes to the trough.

"No, Bull Calf!" I follow him.

At the trough, the cows are snapping their tails stiffly from side to side but none of them drink. I look in. The trough has run dry and only silts line the bottom. The cows peer in and pull out over and over as if their eyes had mistaken the nothingness for water flow. Bull Calf places his head in the trough and tongues at the silt.

A gun fires and all us cows startle. A man swings the pasture gate open and saddles up on his horse. The farmer follows behind on horseback with his boy tucked tight in the saddle.

"Yah, yah, yah, cows!" the man shouts, firing his rifle

into the air again. "Git along, cows, git along!"

The cows back away as the farmer and his man approach the trough. They stop their horses and climb down from the saddles. The boy sits high on the horse, alone. The man slings his rifle over his shoulder, and the farmer hands him the reins.

"You got 'em both?"

"Sure do," says the man.

"Now you hang on tight up there, Jacques," the farmer says patting the boy's leg. "Don't be coming down from that horse, cows are unpredictable animals. I'm just going to clear these pipes and flush the valve. That should get it going again."

"'K, Paw."

"'K, son."

The farmer lifts a tool bag from the horse and throws it to the ground. He kneels, reaches into the sack, and pulls out a wrench. He knocks it against the piping under the trough and the cows back off more.

"Unghf," they cry.

I turn to them. I move my mouth, clatter my teeth together, twist my tongue, and show them my gums. "Listen to me, cows. Men are animals of the most murderous nature. I've seen it myself in the birch-wood building close to where they bring the sun down. In there, men will rip off your hides. They will carve you to your bones. They will hollow your core. Your young will have their throats slit and heads removed at the hands of these men. Hear me, cows! Hear what I am telling you! Run with me, cows, run with me this day or be killed by them on another!"

I press my hide into Bull Calf and plant my hooves into the ground. I hunch my shoulders. Updown, updown, up-down, I move my head. "Cows, let's crash down these fences and run to grasses to call our own." I shake my head side to side and hoof grass over my back.

"Farmer," the man says, "one of them bulls ain't right. He's acting all uppity."

"Which one?" the farmer says, rising.

"That one."

"He's tame," the farmer says, and bends to work again. "I reckon he's out of sorts on account of the water. But he's tame."

"Run with me, cows. Run with me, cows. Run with me, cows!" I lower my head, and I charge the herd.

They cry out in protest but are slow to step out of my way. They don't fear my charge.

"Hey . . . Farmer . . . "

"Paw?"

"Let's trample these men and batter their fences." I

charge the herd, but again the cows move slowly. "I cannot do this alone. Cows, hear me. I am a cow too. I am a bull. I am just like you. Hear me. Listen to me. Charge with me. Run with me!"

I charge them over and over, but with no horns on my head most cows pay me little notice, and soon my legs tire, growing heavy and slow. I look to the hill in the center of the pasture where I first laid down by My Cow's side. I leave the herd and walk to the hill, and being the fine calf he is, Bull Calf follows me.

"Yeah?" the farmer says. "What's that bull up to?"

"Nothing, he's gone. The bull's gone."

At the top of the hill I stand by the dead oak tree with Bull Calf by my side and see all the cows on the pasture.

"This is where I met your mother. It rained so hard all the other cows disappeared."

From here I can look down on the farmer with ease. He is on his back under the trough working on its piping. The boy sits in the saddle petting the horse's mane and playing like he's riding. The man holding the horses' reins looks up at us and then turns his face away. He sees us for certain. The dogs are sleeping in the sunshine between the house and the stable, some of them belly up, and the pups dig their noses under their bitch's belly. Bull Calf looks off to the woods, off to the farthest reaches of the fences, and off to the green grasses growing beyond them. He blinks, bends to chew, but there are no grasses here.

"I was alone and your mother wrapped her neck around my head."

Bull Calf tongues at the dirt.

I step back and place my head against the oak. It has neither warmth nor cold. I wrap my neck around its trunk and hold it tight for as long as I can.

"When I had horns I gored at this trunk and splintered this wood."

Bull Calf flicks his ears, watching me. I step back. Plant my hooves in the ground. Updown, updown, updown, I move my head and hunch my shoulders. I hoof at the dirt and throw it clear over my back. I shake my head terribly from side to side and I snort. "Unghf," I say. "Unghf!"

I charge at the tree and slam my brow into the trunk. It cracks, and twigs rain on my back. I step away, lower my head, hunch my shoulders, and charge again. I grunt when I strike. The tree cracks once more. I buck my body against its bark, and batter the trunk from all sides. The wood splinters all around me. I charge once more and the dead tree splits through its middle and falls to the ground. I pounce on its branches, snapping them to tiny pieces under the weight of my hooves. A tremendous branch forked into two sharp prongs lies near the trunk. I pick it up in my mouth, sink my teeth into its bark, and hoist the branches to the sky like massive horns. I charge down the hill toward the herd, and Bull Calf charges right down after me.

"Bull, Farmer! The bull!"

The man fires his gun when I race into the herd cutting them in two. I charge this way, then that way, then this way again, and all the cows fear me. I try to gore them with the oak's pointy branches. They leap and buck out of my way with their tails down and ears flat.

"Whoa cows, whoa cows, whoa cows!" the man says and blasts the rifle again. This makes the cows run faster.

Soon all the cows are running angry. Bulls charge bulls, cows charge bulls, and all cows charge calves. With one hand on the rifle, the farmer's man tries to steady the horses, but the horses are spooked and they snap him to the ground.

"Jacques!" the farmer screams and wrestles for the reins in the grass. But both horses run off, and the farmer is soon swallowed by the stampede.

"Paw!" the boy shouts as the horse races away with him in the saddle.

"Jacques!"

The farmer's man climbs to his feet, and I barrel into him, sending his rifle into the air. I drop the branch from my mouth and charge after the boy's horse.

"Paw!"

"Neheheheh!" the horse is surrounded by storming cows. He kicks his hind legs into the air and the boy is tossed off.

I slam my way through the pack, battering cow bodies to each side. I keep my head low and look for the boy through all the rampaging hooves. The boy is curled in the kale with his arms shielding his head, his blond hair flecked with flying soil. I buck and kick and press my bull body forward. When I reach the boy, he is weeping.

I hear the farmer shout in the distance. "Jacques!"

I straddle the boy, burying him in my shadow. I plant my hooves firmly into the ground and lower my head. I shake it side to side. Cows come at me from this way, and that way, with their heads pummeling my flanks and horns thrashing at my sides. But still I stand my ground protecting the boy.

"Paw!" he shouts.

A bull charges me and I meet him head on. The force of it all rattles my spine. I look down at the boy.

"Paw!"

"Say my name."

"Paw!"

"Say my name."

The boy does not answer me. With his arms folded in mantis position he cries for his father, even as I loom above him. I reckon he's got no use for singing in such a sorry place, cowering like he is under the weight of my shadow. Still, I protect him.

"Say my name," I ask him again, but the boy takes one look at my ugly cow head and turns away. To him I am incomprehensible.

"Paw!" he cries. He knows nothing of cows and even less of me. This much I know now. I step back and the boy squints in the sunlight. Bulls will be bulls, the farmer says, and I am a bull and nothing less.

"Say my name," I ask once more, and when the boy does not answer, I stomp one of my front hooves into his head.

"OW! No! Help, Paw!" he yells.

The boy raises his hands to cover his face, and I stomp again, cutting his lips.

"Paw!"

"Jacques!"

I drive one of my hooves into his chest. "Say my name."

"Ooomph!" the boy says and coughs, spitting blood onto the kale leaves.

I drive my hoof into his chest again.

"Ooomph, ehhhh, Paw."

I step back. The cows are still swirling around us. I shift my weight onto my hind legs, I bend my knees, and I raise my chest high into the air. For a moment I am standing—on two legs—like a man. Then my bull body crashes down, and I slam both of my front hooves into the boy's chest. His bones snap.

"Jacques!" the farmer screams.

The boy's eyes roll back in his head and they dim.

"Say my name!" I stand on my hind legs once more, wait to gather force, and then slam into the boy one more time.

"Unghf," the boy says. Then he is dead.

Some of the other cows had stopped charging and watched me kill the boy—so did Bull Calf. I turn away from the farmer and his lifeless son, and I lead Bull Calf to the back fence, my hooves leaving a trail of blood in the grass for him and the others to follow.

Bull Calf refuses to climb through the hole in the fence, so I step on the bottom wire with both of my hooves and wedge my shoulders under the top. I push up. The top wire slides up my neck and slices into my hide. I push again. The wires bow around me, but they will not give.

In the distance I hear the farmer wailing about his dead boy. Most of the cows are still charging one another, but several of the cows who watched me crush the boy followed us here. Now, they watch as I try to break the fence.

I push but the wires will not budge, and I am too big to fit.

"We've got to get out of here or the farmer will slaughter us both."

I push again. My front hooves swing on the bottom wire. I hear a faint crack in the fence post. I swing out once more, and I hear it again. I step off the wire and push my head into the fence post. It gives way, its wood weakened with age, rot, and likely wood ants. With one charge, I slam my bull body into the post, sending the entire section of fence twisting and splintering to the ground.

I step over the wires and walk to the edge of the woods,

and Bull Calf follows. We turn and look back at the other cows watching from the pasture. They snap their tails stiffly from side to side, and snort. They flick their ears, trying to make sense of us and the downed fence. Open fences are something they have never known. I walk in and out of the pasture again to show them how. Still they don't follow.

"Cows, hear me. Follow me. Follow me into these woods where the farmer's blade will never find your neck. Follow me into this darkness where the sun of mankind will never scorch your back. Follow me from this pasture, follow me from the tyranny of these grasses, follow me, and fill your faces with wildflower for the rest of your days. Come with me, cows, and live!"

A lone heifer, patched brown and white, steps forward and stops at the edge of the pasture, planting her hooves just beside the fence post. She looks at me, then at Bull Calf, then at the pile of bent wire and shattered wood. Her eyes are dim. She bends and snatches grass into her mouth and chews it, never coming any farther.

I turn and step into the flowering nightshade and bramble. Weeds coil around my hooves, snaring them and cutting up my legs. I rip them from their roots and push forward, making a trail for Bull Calf. I walk between the purple ash and dogwood trees, and he follows right behind. With each step into the heart of the woods, the light recedes behind us, and I think about the cows on the pasture and how we must have looked to them—two cows climbing like jackals into the dark.

Roots curl out of the ground like buried snakes. My hooves slip on a knot of wood and my chest slams into the ground. Bull Calf is much smaller and a bit more sure-footed than I am, but even he is not having an easy go at it. We rest under a dogwood and chew the wild grass between the thickets—the grass is thin but tasty. The sun on the pasture has been put down and the woods darken around us. I don't rightly know how to bring the sun up or get it down from the sky at night. The farmer and his men have done that kind of thing for us cows long as I can remember. For the sake of keeping Bull Calf warm, I reckon I'll just have to figure it out when the time comes—even if it means having to cope in the dark for a while.

Bull Calf plucks flowers from a nightshade bush, and once its branches are bare, he swallows the petals whole. The tree tops have thinned overhead and beams of moonlight break through the branches, casting shadows like slashes across Bull Calf's hide. There are no fireflies to light the way, and in the dark, I close my eyes and I listen to the coyotes yowl.

"We can sleep here, Bull Calf."

I fold my legs and flop to the ground. I lick the dried blood from my forelegs and hooves; it tastes like steel railing on my tongue. There is plenty of room for two cows in this clearing, but Bull Calf doesn't lie next to me no matter how I coax him. He snaps his tail and flicks his ears, staring back along the path we've carved in the woods. He snorts. He's longing for the kale. He's longing for the grass. He's longing for the biggest trapping of pasture life—the familiar. But there can be no going back for us, and I reckon he will never understand this.

The trees don't do much to shelter us from the howling winds. Leaves whirl around our hooves, and Bull Calf's legs start trembling. I'm not sure if he is cold or tired. I rise and press my hide into his. I wrap my neck over his head. Bull Calf teeters and begins to sway. He is tired. His legs buckle and he falls to the ground. I flatten the brush around him and lay by his side.

The woods are dark and quiet. Bull Calf startles me from sleep. He is retching on the forest floor by my side. "Unghf," he says.

"Everything will be better."

"Unghf." He retches again, and then vomits bile and white nightshade petals into the thatch.

The sun's rays are split by the branches curling over my head, and for a moment I think the men have found us here. It is a new morning. The blue birds flutter in the treetops from nest to nest. I leap to my legs and shake my head clear. Bull Calf stirs below me and squints at the light. I flick my ears and listen. I don't hear the men, or the dogs, or the horses. I turn to Bull Calf.

"Bull Calf, my calf, do you see the light? Do you see the sun?"

He does not answer.

"The sun, Bull Calf. Look closely at the sun. This is the same sun that rises over the pasture. I am telling you I'd know its yellow warmth anywhere. We all rise to the same sun, Bull Calf. Cows and men wake to the same sun, and its rays heat us the same. Isn't that a glorious notion?

The sun knows no cows and it knows no men. The sun just is—like the ground we sleep on and the grasses we chew. Let's find where the sun comes up, Bull Calf. Let's press on, and we will find pastures we can call our own. I am certain of this now."

Bull Calf rises and we walk toward the climbing sun, deeper into the woods. We clamber over stones, up hills, and weave our way through the dogwoods, oaks, and ash for most of the day. When the sun is highest over our heads, it's hard to tell where it rose from in the first place with the woods being so dense. We stop to chew, sampling all the wildflowers and onion grasses, but we stay clear of the nightshade. We walk again, keeping the sun at our hinds and reach a horse trail tunneling under massive arms of oaks and magnolias. The trail is soft on our hooves and lined with shrub. The walking is easier here, and we cover lots of ground.

"This will get us there faster, Bull Calf."

The squirrels race up the trees as we hoof by and the weasels go up on their hind legs to get a good look. I figure they've never seen a sight like us before; a bull and his bull calf without fences walking the woods. I snort loudly at them when we pass, and they scatter.

From time to time, Bull Calf lopes in front of me and circles back around nosing at my flank. He bucks, kick-

ing his hind legs into the air and hoofs at the ground, sending leaves and wood chips over his back. Looking at him in this way he hardly seems a calf to me anymore and more like a small bull. His legs are thick, his shoulders are wide, and a hump is gently rising between them on his back.

As the sun lowers in the sky, the clouds are painted like brilliant floating rose petals. I hear the call of geese echo through the timbers. Where there are geese there is water, this much I know. There's a creek in these woods, and if I listen close, I can hear the water bubble against the rocks. We walk some more, the trail curves and leads us to its bank. We drink until our thirst is quenched and we sleep.

"That's what he said to me."

It's a man's voice, none I recognize. Then there's another man.

"Well I guess I would have done the same thing then. But really you couldn't make the right decision here. You were damned if you did and damned if you didn't."

"Uh huh."

I push my body up and wake Bull Calf. The men's

voices are getting louder. They are getting closer to us. Bull Calf sees my ears flatten and tail stiffen down. He does the same. I push my hind into the shrubs as far back from the trail edge as I can, and Bull Calf follows me in. We stand motionless in marshy grass close to the creek bank and wait for the men to pass. Bull Calf snorts, shakes his head. Bulls can be unpredictable creatures, and bull calves even more so, and I fear he might charge them.

Through the brush I see two men on horseback come from around the bend. They are not farming men, I can tell by the dress, and they are not riding fast. All this makes me feel less anxious. We wait until they ride their horses down the trail and disappear. Bull Calf and I climb from the brush, and after making sure the trail is clear, we walk again, keeping the creek on our side.

Bull Calf is limping, favoring one of his front hooves, and his walking slows. I suppose he just might have hurt himself on the rocks, or roots, or tree trunks we've climbed over. There've been many. My hooves hurt too, even my legs ache up to my hips and shoulders. But I fear Bull Calf could be coming down with lameness. Lame cows always start with a limp. Back on the pasture there were many times the lameness would get so bad the farmer would have to put the cow down.

We walk farther down the trail, stopping on occasion to let Bull Calf rest his hoof. As the sky darkens around us, his limp is getting worse and when he stops walking he lifts it off the ground. Still he tries his best to follow.

"You're a fine calf, Bull Calf. Soon we will find our own pasture and you can rest for days. I will bring you grass and brush and wildflower and lay it under your mouth, just like I did when you were young."

Bull Calf lunges forward, following me, and as soon as dusk becomes dark, the coyotes pounce on him.

Bull Calf cries out to me, "Unghf!"

Four coyotes are digging their paws into Bull Calf's hide and sinking their sharp teeth into his flesh; one up on his haunches, two at his neck, and one down by his bad hoof. He is bucking, kicking, and crying, struggling to get free. But the coyotes got him good and locked in their jaws. Three other coyotes circle the attack, snarling and bearing their teeth. I pounce on them, and one of them lunges at me, clamping its jaws around my throat. Then the other digs his fangs into my shoulder. The last coyote goes for my flank. I swing my whole bull body around, throwing them off. I lower my head and charge, but I have no horns to gore them with. One of the coyotes bites into my hind. I kick him with my rear hoof, sending him flying into the brush where he lands with a yelp. Before he can get up, I stomp on him and shatter his legs. He wails and drags himself into the woods. The other two coyotes come at me again, and I stomp them to the ground too; they both run off bloodied.

I charge the remaining coyotes and pry them one by one from Bull Calf. He is bleeding and he presses his hide against mine. He horns at the ground and shakes his head side to side. Updown, updown, updown, he snorts and then charges right for the largest coyote, goring it on his tiny horns. With the flick of his head, he tosses the coyote into the air. The coyote lands by my hooves, and I stomp on him. He yelps and scrambles to his feet and races under the brush.

The other coyotes back away, snarling at us. They lower their haunches and flatten their ears against their heads. We charge them together and they disappear.

"We have beaten the dogs, Bull Calf, we have beaten the dogs!"

Bull Calf folds into the brush, and I stand over him licking the wounds along his back and neck. I fold down beside him. His front hoof is swollen. I press my lips against it, and it is warm—lameness has taken hold. Bull Calf pulls his hoof away and tucks it close to his chest. We sleep.

We have walked most of the day along the trail, and Bull Calf's limp has worsened some more. We rest in the warmth of the sun. His whole front leg is swollen down to his hoof and soon he no longer places it on the ground when he walks. He jerks forward on three legs, still following me best he can. There is a small clearing of pastureland off the trail through the trees, with rolling green grass that climbs to a cliff.

"Bull Calf, if you can make it to that cliff I can show you the world. I reckon there are pastures untouched by cows just waiting to be devoured. They can be our pastures—every single one of them. With time more cows will come. I'm not sure when, or how many cows will come, but one day I know they will come. When they do, we will welcome them to our home, Bull Calf. We will invite them to chew with us on the wild flowers. In the warm seasons we will eat hibiscus and in cold season we'll stuff our cheeks with chicory. We will all live together without fences and without farmers and without feed. Just through these woods and you will see a world where we can be free to control our own lives; where we don't wait for the farmer's knife."

I step off the trail and over thickets into the forest, but Bull Calf does not follow me. I turn to him, flick my ears, and snort. He blinks and lowers his head. He searches the length of the trail one way, then down the other way.

"I will not leave you. We can stay on the trail if that is what you wish."

With his bad hoof hanging by his chest, Bull Calf moves his hind legs forward, bracing himself, and then throws his body toward me, landing on his good front hoof with a thud. He jerks back on his hind legs and wobbles forward again. He climbs into the woods teetering over roots, around trees, and over shrubs and slowly hobbles to my side. We walk toward the clearing.

Starlings dance in the treetops, singing to each other. A white-tailed doe jumps out of the brush and zigzags away through the trees. A massive buck follows her. He's about as wide as me only much taller. He stops to look at us. We stop. We look at him. We study each other for a while. His horns are extraordinary, forking and twisting over his head like the branches of a magnificent oak. I've never seen a bull with horns like that and I doubt there ever was one. I feel shamed. I lower my head and flatten my ears. Bull Calf does the same. The buck snorts and bounds off across the trail and through the forest with hardly a sound at all. I continue toward the clearing with Bull Calf lurching behind me.

After a few labored steps, Bull Calf crashes to the ground and rolls on his side. "Unghf," he cries.

"Get up, Bull Calf, the clearing is within our reach. A few more steps we'll be on the grassy pasture. You can eat every blade of grass on it; I won't have a bite. The cliff will show us all the lands the world has to offer cows. They will be our lands. Get up, Bull Calf, get up and come see this with me."

Bull Calf does not get up. His breathing is fast, faint, and his tongue is pale and dry. His eyes are dimming. I fear the lameness has spread, which it is known to do. I look to the clearing, flick my ears, and look down on Bull Calf. I race out of the woods and gather grasses and wild-flowers in my cheeks and lay them under his snout, but Bull Calf will not eat.

I force all the air out my chest. "I am here, Bull Calf. I will never leave your side."

I fold to the floor and lie next to him, resting my chin over his horns. I move my mouth, roll my tongue, show my teeth, and sing.

> *Dodo, l'enfant do,*
> *l'enfant dormira bien vite,*
> *dodo, l'enfant do,*
> *l'enfant dormira bientôt.*

Une poule blanche,
est là dans la grange.
Qui va faire un petit coco
pour l'enfant qui va faire dodo.

Tout le monde est sage,
dans le voisinage.
Il est l'heure d'aller dormir,
le sommeil va bientôt venir. *

When Bull Calf closes his eyes I stop singing and lay my head next to his.

I fill my belly with milk at my mother's teat. All the cows are still, watching me, marveling at me. They watch me run, they watch me kick, and they watch me hoof at the ground. My mother licks my brow and gnaws at my hair. She pushes her cheek into mine and rubs. We chew grass next to each other. When she tires of grazing she lies in the sun. I press my ear against her hide, and I hear Bull Calf charging inside her chest.

* For English translation see page 130.

I wake, but I cannot wake Bull Calf. I nudge his head with my mouth, and he does not stir. Each breath is short, loud, and sharp. Sometimes he'll stop breathing only to start again. His eyes shine like water but are black like tar. His limbs flop loose like rope. I lick his brow.

"I never told you the most important secret I know about cows, Bull Calf. There is a lush green pasture where all the cows are free, as they should be. You can see it just beyond this cliff. It's called India. I overheard the farmer and his men talking about it. They said the gods protect the cows because the cows protect the children. Imagine that! Cows are the most supreme of all animals! I reckon I might have angered the gods for killing the farmer's boy back on the pasture and that's why your foot got lame. For that I am at your mercy, Bull Calf, but I was protecting you. The men would have killed you in a season, perhaps sooner. They would have sliced you to pieces. I could not let them do that. You are my child. You are the only world I got. So in a sense, I've done what I've been asked. Please forgive my bullish nature. Sometimes right and wrong are part of the same thing. It seems unlikely but it's true."

Bull Calf stops breathing.

"Bull Calf! There is one more thing I want to tell you."

He gasps and breathes again.

"être," I whisper in his ear, "that is my name."

Bull Calf is heavy, and I use my head to slide his lifeless body under an oak tree. I snatch chicory and bramble in my teeth and lay it over him so the buzzards can never pick on his flesh. "You are a fine calf, Bull Calf, and the finest memory of my pasture life." I leave him in the woods and step out into the sundrenched grasses. I bend to chew the grass and it is tasteless. The starlings flock from the trees and fly across the sky like a swirling black cloud.

I walk to the cliff and look over the edge. Below me, as far as my eyes can see, thousands and thousands of cows are chewing grasses in pastures lined with fences.

aftêrword

Sometimes I think it may be best not to reckon like I do—instead of looking outside the fences, it might serve me well to stay looking inside. Better yet, it would be nice to not consider the fences at all. I suppose that's how most cows deal with them. I don't rightly know how to go about doing that. I see pastures and fences for what they are, and I see them for what they make me. Most cows have no sense about these things, but it's a wrong thing to fight your sensibilities once you have them. This much I know.

After the cliff I walked back into the woods, knelt by Bull Calf's body for a while and asked him to forgive me one more time. Then I wandered in the woods, onto the trail with no particular direction in mind. I sat in the creek and let the lily pads wash around me. I drank its water, and drank again. I chewed on the forest bramble, chicory, hoptree, and even nightshade from time to time, often mixing the flowers in my mouth with the onion grass so I don't get sick. I followed the moon in the dark and dreamt I had terrific horns like a buck night after night. What I'd do with horns like that, I reckon I'll never know. I do know this, though. A cow can figure a life in the woods and on the strips of land that lay between the pastures, but it is fiercely lonesome.

"Unghf," I say.

I weave between the dogwoods and purple ash. I step over the bramble and nightshade and step out of the woods into the sunlight. New hardwood posts have been set all along the back fence, and the hole I tore in the wires has been repaired.

I poke my face through the fence wires and into the pasture. The cows are filling their bellies on kale and green grasses. The calves are drinking the milk of their mothers. The dogs are sleeping and the horses are in the stable. In the distance, the farmer's men are herding cows into the chute, and at the top of the hill the fallen oak trunk has weeds sprouting from its wood.

I pull my head out of the pasture and the top wire slices into my ear. When the pain subsides, I bend and stuff my cheeks full with daffodils.

French/English Translations

Pages 7–8, 76

French	English
French	**English**
Alouette, gentille Alouette	Skylark, nice skylark
Alouette—je te plumerai	Skylark—I shall pluck you
Alouette, gentille Alouette	Skylark, nice skylark
Alouette—je te plumerai	Skylark—I shall pluck you.
Je te plumerai la tête	I shall pluck your head
Et la tête, et la tête	And your head, and your head
Et le nez, et le nez	And your nose, and your nose
Alouette—je te plumerai	Skylark—I shall pluck you

Pages 36–37

French	English
French	**English**
Frère Jacques, Frère Jacques	Brother Jacques, Brother Jacques
Dormez-vous? Dormez-vous?	Are you sleeping? Are you sleeping?
Sonnez les matines	Morning bells are ringing
Sonnez les matines	Morning bells are ringing

Ding, dong, ding—ding, dong, ding

Pages 53, 123–124

French	**English**
Dodo, l'enfant do,	Lullaby, child, lullaby
l'enfant dormira bien vite,	The child will go to sleep quickly
dodo, l'enfant do,	Lullaby, child, lullaby
Une poule blanche,	A white hen
est là dans la grange.	Is there in the barn
Qui va faire un petit coco	It will lay an egg
pour l'enfant qui va-faire dodo.	For the child who will fall asleep
Tout le monde est sage	All the world is wise
dans le voisinage.	In the neighborhood
Il est l'heure d'aller dormir,	It is time to go to sleep
le sommeil va bientôt venir.	Sleep will soon be here

reading group questions

1. In French the verb "être" means "to be" or "to exist." In the novel, "être" is the name of the protagonist cow, but also the only word he can say aloud. Discuss the implications of this. Is être struggling for existence, understanding, significance, or all three?

2. *être the cow* is an allegory, in the tradition of George Orwell's classic 1945 novella *Animal Farm*. While *Animal Farm* serves as an indictment of totalitarian regimes, *être the cow* uses allegory to critique contemporary society. Written during the recession of 2008 and 2009, discuss the social, political and economic context that *être the cow* is responding to.

3. On the first page, être says the pasture is more crowded than ever, and "all the good grasses been chewed long ago and now we only have yellowed patches to fill our bellies." This statement is followed by the solitary sentence, "I haven't eaten a daffodil in several seasons." Why is this sentence standing alone? Daffodils, also called *Narcissus* plants, can be toxic and intoxicating to cows. Explore the meaning of the daffodil in this story, and why does être stuff his cheeks full with daffodils in the final scene?

4. In the story, être struggles with the decision to accept his fate as a cow or challenge his destiny. Only when he witnesses the carnage in the slaughterhouse does être realize the grave consequences of cow life. How does the slaughterhouse change être's perspective?

5. Powerlessness and shame are dominant themes in *être the cow*. How are these two sentiments depicted in the story? How do they serve to propel être's search for understanding and significance?

6. On the pasture, être is frustrated by his inability to communicate

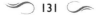

with other cows and the people at Gorwell Farm. Among the cows he is alone in his self-awareness. Why is this? What message do you think être would like to convey to the other cows? What message do you think he wishes to communicate to the farmer and the farmer's boy?

7. Many of the sounds and songs in *être the cow* are familiar, yet unfamiliar. The cows don't say "moo" but instead say "unghf" or "anghf." The barking of the dogs is not written as "bow-wow" or "arf" but instead as "owf." The lullabies the boy sings are in French, yet they are recognized by most Americans. Why is this "familiar yet unfamiliar" device used and what does it suggest?

8. être can only say one word, his name. He tells the reader his name in the opening pages of *être the cow*. He shouts "être" to the other cows after his first encounter with Black Bull. He tells the boy his name, and later, during the stampede, être commands the boy to say his name. Finally, as Bull Calf is dying in the woods, être reveals his name to him. Why does être do this?

9. The violence and brutality of nature features prominently in the novel—ants carry a disembodied mantis head and "cut the weevils to pieces," the egrets feast on the earthworms, and "the barn owls swoop and snatch mice from the grass to feed their young." Black Bull gores another bull's calf to death. But the book draws a line between the innocent violence of nature and the senseless violence of man. Jacques, the farmer's boy, tosses stones against être's body, the farmer's men shoot a lame cow execution-style in the middle of the pasture, and in the slaughterhouse cows are killed by men without mercy, then sawed and sliced to pieces. How does the violence of man and the violence of nature differ in the story, and was être's killing Jacques an act of innocent or senseless violence?

10. After witnessing the slaughter of cows in the birch-wood building être has a series of revelations about his pasture life. While he used to think men hid their skins under hats and clothing because they were "just ashamed of their uneven wiry patches of hair, or the lack of tails on their hinds, or the lack of horns on their heads," he then realizes "it's the blood." The chickens, "born with wings that will never fly," are no longer the lowest animals on the farm, because cows "are born with legs that can't outrun dogs, eyes that don't weep, and a mouth that doesn't shout, but only eats." Discuss these revelations. How do they change être's worldview? How do they change his mission?

11. Because être the cow is a fable, it relies on metaphor and symbolism to give the characters and setting a higher significance. For instance the oak tree, which is often used by authors as a symbolic "tree of life," is dead with bare branches in this story, yet it is instrumental in être's struggle. When Farmer Creely and his son, Jacques, are first introduced, the farmer says, "We got to feed the pigs first, Jacques . . . pigs come first." What or who do the pigs symbolize? Discuss the use of symbolism in the story. How are the grass, the pasture fence, Black Bull, My Cow, Bull Calf, the horns of bulls and the buck, and the slaughterhouse used as metaphor?

12. A dog is well known to be man's best friend, and in être the cow, the dogs taunt the pasture cows "without mercy." Explore the relationship between the men and the dogs at Gorwell Farm. Later être and Bull Calf triumph over coyotes while walking in the woods. être proclaims, "We have beaten the dogs!" Why is this victory important?

about the author

Sean Kenniff is neither a cow nor a vegetarian. The author of *Stop *Effing Yourself*, he is a physician, television journalist, and radio host. In 2000 he was one of the original castaways on the CBS reality show *Survivor!* Born and raised in New York and now living in Miami, Florida, he was working for a large U.S. corporation during the recession of 2009 when his position was suddenly eliminated. He went to live with the cows.

Être the Cow is his first novella.